Edwidge Danticat

CREATE DANGEROUSLY

Edwidge Danticat is the author of numerous books, including *Brother, I'm Dying,* which won the National Book Critics Circle Award and was a National Book Award finalist; *Breath, Eyes, Memory,* an Oprah Book Club selection; *Krik? Krak!,* a National Book Award finalist; *The Farming of Bones,* an American Book Award winner; and *The Dew Breaker,* a PEN/Faulkner Award finalist and winner of the inaugural Story Prize. She lives in Miami with her husband and two daughters.

ALSO BY EDWIDGE DANTICAT

Fiction

The Dew Breaker
The Farming of Bones
Krik? Krak!
Breath, Eyes, Memory

Nonfiction

Brother, I'm Dying
After the Dance: A Walk Through Carnival in Jacmel, Haiti

For Young Readers

Eight Days: A Story of Haiti
Anacaona, Golden Flower
Behind the Mountains

CREATE DANGEROUSLY

CREATE DANGEROUSLY

The Immigrant Artist at Work

Edwidge Danticat

Vintage Books
A Division of Random House, Inc.
New York

FIRST VINTAGE BOOKS EDITION, SEPTEMBER 2011

Library of Congress Cataloging-in-Publication Data
Danticat, Edwidge, 1969–
Create dangerously : the immigrant artist at work / Edwidge Danticat.
—1st Vintage Books ed.
p. cm.
Includes bibliographical references and index.
1. Danticat, Edwidge, 1969–
2. Authors, American—20th century—Biography.
3. Emigration and immigration. 4. Expatriate artists—United States.
5. Artists—Haiti. 6. Haiti—Social conditions—20th century.
I. Title.
PS3554.A5815Z463 2011
813'.54—dc22
[B]
2011016568

Vintage ISBN: 978-0-307-94643-0

www.vintagebooks.com

Printed in the United States of America
10   9   8

two hundred thousand and more

This is the fiction of beginnings, couched in the past tense. But the chants are not *in memoriam*. They may be heard as a celebration of each contemporary recapitulation of that first creation.

—Maya Deren, *Divine Horsemen: The Living Gods of Haiti*

CONTENTS

CONTENTS

CREATE DANGEROUSLY

Create Dangerously: The Immigrant Artist at Work

On November 12, 1964, in Port-au-Prince, Haiti, a huge crowd gathered to witness an execution. The president of Haiti at that time was the dictator François "Papa Doc" Duvalier, who was seven years into what would be a fifteen-year term. On the day of the execution, he decreed that government offices be closed so that hundreds of state employees could be in the crowd. Schools were shut down and principals ordered to bring their students. Hundreds of people from outside the capital were bused in to watch.

The two men to be executed were Marcel Numa and Louis Drouin. Marcel Numa was a tall, dark-skinned twenty-one-year-old. He was from a family of coffee planters in a beautiful southern Haitian town called Jérémie, which is often dubbed the "city of poets." Numa had studied engineering at the Bronx Merchant Academy in New York and had worked for an American shipping company.

Louis Drouin, nicknamed Milou, was a thirty-one-year-old light-skinned man who was also from Jérémie. He had served in the U.S. army—at Fort Knox, and then at Fort Dix in New Jersey—and had studied finance before working for French,

Swiss, and American banks in New York. Marcel Numa and Louis Drouin had been childhood friends in Jérémie.

The men had remained friends when they'd both moved to New York in the 1950s, after François Duvalier came to power. There they had joined a group called Jeune Haiti, or Young Haiti, and were two of thirteen Haitians who left the United States for Haiti in 1964 to engage in a guerrilla war that they hoped would eventually topple the Duvalier dictatorship.

The men of Jeune Haiti spent three months fighting in the hills and mountains of southern Haiti and eventually most of them died in battle. Marcel Numa was captured by members of Duvalier's army while he was shopping for food in an open market, dressed as a peasant. Louis Drouin was wounded in battle and asked his friends to leave him behind in the woods.

"According to our principles I should have committed suicide in that situation," Drouin reportedly declared in a final statement at his secret military trial. "Chandler and Guerdès [two other Jeune Haiti members] were wounded . . . the first one asked . . . his best friend to finish him off; the second committed suicide after destroying a case of ammunition and all the documents. That did not affect me. I reacted only after the disappearance of Marcel Numa, who had been sent to look for food and for some means of escape by sea. We were very close and our parents were friends."

After months of attempting to capture the men of Jeune Haiti and after imprisoning and murdering hundreds of their relatives, Papa Doc Duvalier wanted to make a spectacle of Numa and Drouin's deaths.

So on November 12, 1964, two pine poles are erected outside the national cemetery. A captive audience is gathered.

Radio, print, and television journalists are summoned. Numa and Drouin are dressed in what on old black-and-white film seems to be the clothes in which they'd been captured—khakis for Drouin and a modest white shirt and denim-looking pants for Numa. They are both marched from the edge of the crowd toward the poles. Their hands are tied behind their backs by two of Duvalier's private henchmen, Tonton Macoutes in dark glasses and civilian dress. The Tonton Macoutes then tie the ropes around the men's biceps to bind them to the poles and keep them upright.

Numa, the taller and thinner of the two, stands erect, in perfect profile, barely leaning against the square piece of wood behind him. Drouin, who wears brow-line eyeglasses, looks down into the film camera that is taping his final moments. Drouin looks as though he is fighting back tears as he stands there, strapped to the pole, slightly slanted. Drouin's arms are shorter than Numa's and the rope appears looser on Drouin. While Numa looks straight ahead, Drouin pushes his head back now and then to rest it on the pole.

Time is slightly compressed on the copy of the film I have and in some places the images skip. There is no sound. A large crowd stretches out far beyond the cement wall behind the bound Numa and Drouin. To the side is a balcony filled with schoolchildren. Some time elapses, it seems, as the school-children and others mill around. The soldiers shift their guns from one hand to the other. Some audience members shield their faces from the sun by raising their hands to their fore-heads. Some sit idly on a low stone wall.

A young white priest in a long robe walks out of the crowd with a prayer book in his hands. It seems that he is the person everyone has been waiting for. The priest says a few words to Drouin, who slides his body upward in a defiant pose. Drouin motions with his head toward his friend. The priest spends a little more time with Numa, who bobs his head as the priest speaks. If this is Numa's extreme unction, it is an abridged version.

The priest then returns to Drouin and is joined there by a stout Macoute in plain clothes and by two uniformed policemen, who lean in to listen to what the priest is saying to Drouin. It is possible that they are all offering Drouin some type of eye or face cover that he's refusing. Drouin shakes his head as if to say, let's get it over with. No blinders or hoods are placed on either man.

The firing squad, seven helmeted men in khaki military uniforms, stretch out their hands on either side of their bodies. They touch each other's shoulders to position and space themselves. The police and army move the crowd back, perhaps to keep them from being hit by ricocheted bullets. The members of the firing squad pick up their Springfield rifles, load their ammunition, and then place their weapons on their shoulders. Off screen someone probably shouts, "Fire!" and they do. Numa and Drouin's heads slump sideways at the same time, showing that the shots have hit home.

When the men's bodies slide down the poles, Numa's arms end up slightly above his shoulders and Drouin's below his. Their heads return to an upright position above their kneeling bodies, until a soldier in camouflage walks over and delivers the final coup de grace, after which their heads slump forward and their bodies slide further toward the bottom of the pole. Blood spills out of Numa's mouth. Drouin's glasses fall to the ground, pieces of blood and brain matter clouding the cracked lenses.

The next day, *Le Matin*, one of the country's national newspapers, described the stunned-looking crowd as "feverish, communicating in a mutual patriotic exaltation to curse adventurism and brigandage."

"The government pamphlets circulating in Port-au-Prince last week left little to the imagination," reported the November 27, 1964, edition of the American newsweekly *Time*. "'Dr. François Duvalier will fulfill his sacrosanct mission. He has crushed and will always crush the attempts of the opposition. Think well, renegades. Here is the fate awaiting you and your kind.'"

All artists, writers among them, have several stories—one might call them creation myths—that haunt and obsess them. This is one of mine. I don't even remember when I first heard about it. I feel as though I have always known it, having filled in the curiosity-driven details through photographs, newspaper and magazine articles, books, and films as I have gotten older.

Like many a creation myth, aside from its heartrending clash of life and death, homeland and exile, the execution of Marcel Numa and Louis Drouin involves a disobeyed directive from a higher authority and a brutal punishment as a result. If we think back to the biggest creation myth of all, the world's very first people, Adam and Eve, disobeyed the superior being that fashioned them out of chaos, defying God's order not to eat what must have been the world's most desirable apple. Adam and Eve were then banished from Eden, resulting in everything from our having to punch a clock to spending many long, painful hours giving birth.

The order given to Adam and Eve was not to eat the apple. Their ultimate punishment was banishment, exile from paradise. We, the storytellers of the world, ought to be more grateful than most that banishment, rather than execution, was chosen for Adam and Eve, for had they been executed, there would never have been another story told, no stories to pass on.

In his play *Caligula*, Albert Camus, from whom I borrow part of the title of this essay, has Caligula, the third Roman emperor, declare that it doesn't matter whether one is exiled or executed, but it is much more important that Caligula has the power to choose. Even before they were executed, Marcel Numa and Louis Drouin had already been exiled. As young men, they had fled Haiti with their parents when Papa Doc Duvalier had come to power in 1957 and had immediately targeted for arrest all his detractors and resistors in the city of poets and elsewhere.

Marcel Numa and Louis Drouin had made new lives for themselves, becoming productive young immigrants in the United States. In addition to his army and finance experience, Louis Drouin was said to have been a good writer and the communications director of Jeune Haiti. In the United States, he contributed to a Haitian political journal called *Lambi*. Marcel Numa was from a family of writers. One of his male relatives, Nono Numa, had adapted the seventeenth-century French playwright Pierre Corneille's *Le Cid*, placing it in a Haitian setting. Many of the young men Numa and Drouin joined with to form Jeune Haiti had had fathers killed by Papa Doc Duvalier, and had returned, Le Cid and Hamlet-like, to revenge them.

Like most creation myths, this one too exists beyond the scope of my own life, yet it still feels present, even urgent. Marcel Numa and Louis Drouin were patriots who died so that other Haitians could live. They were also immigrants, like me. Yet, they had abandoned comfortable lives in the United States and sacrificed themselves for the homeland. One of the first things the despot Duvalier tried to take away from them was the mythic element of their stories. In the propaganda preceding their execution, he labeled them not Haitian, but foreign rebels, good-for-nothing *blans*.

At the time of the execution of Marcel Numa and Louis Drouin, my recently married, twenty-nine-year-old parents lived in Haiti, in a neighborhood called Bel Air, about a thirty-minute walk from the cemetery. Bel Air had a government-sponsored community center, a *centre d'étude*, where young men and women—but mostly young men—went to study in the evenings, especially if they had no electricity at home. Some of these young people—not my parents, but young people who studied at the center—belonged to a book club, a reading group sponsored by the Alliance Française, the French Institute. The book group was called Le Club de Bonne Humeur, or the Good Humor Club. At the time, Le Club de Bonne Humeur was reading Camus' play *Caligula* with an eye to possibly staging it.

In Camus' version of Caligula's life, when Caligula's sister, who is also his lover, dies, Caligula unleashes his rage and slowly unravels. In a preface to an English translation of the play, Camus wrote, "I look in vain for philosophy in these four acts.... I have little regard for an art that deliberately aims to shock because it is unable to convince."

After the executions of Marcel Numa and Louis Drouin, as the images of their deaths played over and over in cinemas and on state-run television, the young men and women of the Club de Bonne Humeur, along with the rest of Haiti, desperately needed art that could convince. They needed art that could convince them that they would not die the same way Numa and Drouin did. They needed to be convinced that words could still be spoken, that stories could still be told and passed on. So, as my father used to tell it, these young people donned white sheets as togas and they tried to stage Camus' play—quietly, quietly—in many of their houses, where they whispered lines like:

> Execution relieves and liberates. It is a universal tonic, just in precept as in practice. A man dies because he is guilty. A man is guilty because he is one of Caligula's subjects. Ergo all men are guilty and shall die. It is only a matter of time and patience.

The legend of the underground staging of this and other plays, clandestine readings of pieces of literature, was so strong that years after Papa Doc Duvalier died, every time there was a political murder in Bel Air, one of the young aspiring intellectuals in the neighborhood where I spent the first twelve years of my life might inevitably say that someone should put on a play. And because the uncle who raised me while my parents were in New York for two-thirds of the first twelve years of my life, because that uncle was a minister in Bel Air and had a church and school with some available space, occasionally some of these plays were read and staged, quietly, quietly, in the backyard of his church.

There were many recurrences of this story throughout the country, book and theater clubs secretly cherishing some potentially subversive piece of literature, families burying if not burning their entire libraries, books that might seem innocent but could easily betray them. Novels with the wrong titles. Treatises with the right titles and intentions. Strings of words that, uttered, written, or read, could cause a person's death. Sometimes these words were written by Haitian writers like Marie Vieux-Chauvet and René Depestre, among others. Other times they were written by foreign or *blan* writers, writers like Aimé Césaire, Frantz Fanon, or Albert Camus, who were untouchable because they were either not Haitian or already long dead. The fact that death prevented one from being banished—unlike, say, the English novelist Graham Greene, who was banned from Haiti after writing *The Comedians*—made the "classic" writers all the more appealing. Unlike the country's own citizens, these writers could neither be tortured or murdered themselves nor cause their family members to be tortured or murdered. And no matter how hard he tried, Papa Doc Duvalier could not make their words go away. Their maxims and phrases would keep coming back, buried deep in memories by the rote recitation techniques that the Haitian school system had taught so well. Because those writers who were still in Haiti, not yet exiled or killed, could not freely perform or print their own words outright, many of them turned, or returned, to the Greeks.

When it was a crime to pick up a bloodied body on the street, Haitian writers introduced Haitian readers to Sophocles' *Oedipus Rex* and *Antigone*, which had been rewritten in Creole and placed in Haitian settings by the playwright Franck

Fouché and the poet Felix Morisseau Leroy. This is where these writers placed their bets, striking a dangerous balance between silence and art.

How do writers and readers find each other under such dangerous circumstances? Reading, like writing, under these conditions is disobedience to a directive in which the reader, our Eve, already knows the possible consequences of eating that apple but takes a bold bite anyway.

How does that reader find the courage to take this bite, open that book? After an arrest, an execution? Of course he or she may find it in the power of the hushed chorus of other readers, but she can also find it in the writer's courage in having stepped forward, in having written, or rewritten, in the first place.

Create dangerously, for people who read dangerously. This is what I've always thought it meant to be a writer. Writing, knowing in part that no matter how trivial your words may seem, someday, somewhere, someone may risk his or her life to read them. Coming from where I come from, with the history I have—having spent the first twelve years of my life under both dictatorships of Papa Doc and his son, Jean-Claude—this is what I've always seen as the unifying principle among all writers. This is what, among other things, might join Albert Camus and Sophocles to Toni Morrison, Alice Walker, Osip Mandelstam, and Ralph Waldo Emerson to Ralph Waldo Ellison. Somewhere, if not now, then maybe years in the future, a future that we may have yet to dream of, someone may risk his or her life to read us. Somewhere, if not now, then maybe years in the future, we may also save someone's life (or mind) because they have given us a passport, making us honorary citizens of their culture.

This is why when I wrote a book called *The Dew Breaker*, a book about a *choukèt lawoze*, or a Duvalier-era torturer, a book that is partly set in the period following the Numa and Drouin executions, I used an epigraph from a poem by Osip Mandelstam, who famously said, "Only in Russia is poetry respected—it gets people killed."

The quotation I used is:

> Maybe this is the beginning of madness . . .
> Forgive me for what I am saying.
> Read it . . . quietly, quietly.

There are many possible interpretations of what it means to create dangerously, and Albert Camus, like the poet Osip Mandelstam, suggests that it is creating as a revolt against silence, creating when both the creation and the reception, the writing and the reading, are dangerous undertakings, disobedience to a directive.

This is a part of my story that I have always wanted to understand better: my family's brief encounters with the pleasures and dangers of reading. I am at a great deficit here because, aside from my much older cousin Maxo, there were not many fanatical readers in my family that I know of, much less people who would risk their lives over a book. Perhaps at a time when one could be shot so easily, assassinated so publicly, not reading or writing was a survival mechanism. Still, sprinkles of other readers' stories continue to intrigue and thrill me. Young men and women who worshipped Euripides and Voltaire, George Sand and Colette and Haiti's own physician novelist, Jacques Stephen Alexis, who in April 1961, three years before Numa and Drouin were executed, had been ambushed and murdered trying to return from exile, some say, to help topple the Duvalier dictatorship.

No one in my family that I know of had witnessed Numa and Drouin's execution in person. Still they could not help, when it came up, talking about it, even if in the broadest of terms.

"It was a very tragic time," my mother now says.

"It was something that touched a generation," my minister uncle used to say.

They were patriots who died so the rest of us could live, is a line I borrowed from my father. My father was the one who, while lying on his deathbed in early 2005, told me about the banned books and the plays. Only when he mentioned togas and Caesars, and an author with a name that sounds like *camion*, did I manage to find my way, among many other possible choices, to Camus' *Caligula*. I could be wrong about this too, making connections only I believe are there.

The only book my parents and uncle have read more than once is the Bible. I used to fear their reading my books, worried about disappointing them. My stories do not hold a candle to having lived under a dictatorship for most of your adult life, to having your neighbors disappear and not being able even to acknowledge it, to being forced to act as though these neighbors had never existed at all. Reading, and perhaps ultimately writing, is nothing like living in a place and time where two very young men are killed in a way that is treated like entertainment.

Mourir est beau, to die is beautiful, declares the Haitian national anthem. But writing could never attain that kind of beauty. Or could it? Writing is nothing like dying in, for, and possibly with, your country.

When I first started returning as a public person, as an "author," to Haiti, a place where people trace your failures and successes along family lines, I was often asked if there were any writers in my family. If there were, I do not know. But another thing that has always haunted and obsessed me is trying to write the things that have always haunted and obsessed those who came before me.

Bel Air, now a destitute and earthquake-ravaged area overlooking Port-au-Prince harbor, was still a poor neighborhood when I was growing up there. But, along with ideological students, our neighborhood also had its intellectuals. The brilliant Haitian novelist/poet/playwright/painter Frankétienne grew up in Bel Air, as did the younger novelist and poet Louis Phillipe Dalembert, who later left for Paris and then Rome. There was also Edner Day, a well-known Macoute, who tried to court one of my young cousins, who tried to court everyone's young cousins. He seemed literary for no other reason than that he was sometimes seen in the afternoons sitting on his balcony reading. But he was also a rumored murderer, one of those who may have shot Numa and Drouin.

In "L'artiste et son temps," translated into English as "Create Dangerously," Camus writes: "Art cannot be a monologue. We are on the high seas. The artist, like everyone else, must bend to his oar, without dying if possible." In many ways, Numa and Drouin shared the destiny of many Haitian artists, particularly that of the physician-novelist Jacques Stephen Alexis, who wrote such beautiful prose that the first time I read his description of freshly baked bread, I raised the book closer to my nose to sniff it. Perhaps there are no writers in my family because they were too busy trying to find bread.

Perhaps there are no writers in my family because they were not allowed to or could barely afford to attend a decrepit village school as children. Perhaps there are no artists in my family because they were silenced by the brutal directives of one dictatorship, or one natural disaster, after another. Perhaps, just as Alice Walker writes of her own forebears in her essay "In Search of Our Mother's Gardens," my blood ancestors—unlike my literary ancestors—were so weather-beaten, terror-stricken, and maimed that they were stifled. As a result, those who somehow managed to create became, in my view, martyrs and saints.

"Instead of being perceived as whole persons," wrote Walker, "their bodies became shrines: what was thought to be their minds became temples suitable for worship. These crazy 'Saints' stared out at the world, wildly, like lunatics—or quietly, like suicides; and the 'God' that was in their gaze was as mute as a great stone."

Of course I could be completely off base. Bel Air's Franké-tienne, among others, somehow managed to remain human and alive in Haiti, before, during, and after the Duvalier dictatorship, producing a massive and innovative body of work. Balancing on the metaphorical high seas and bending to their oars without dying is what the majority of Haitians have always done, generation after generation. This legacy of resilience and survival is what had inspired Jacques Stephen Alexis, Marcel Numa and Louis Drouin, and so many others to sacrifice their lives. Their death is possibly among the shocking incidents that eventually motivated so many others, like my parents, for example, to leave. This may be one of the reasons I live in the United States of America today, writing in this language that is not mine. This could possibly be why I am an immigrant and hopefully an artist, an immigrant artist at work. Even though there is probably no such thing as an immigrant artist in this globalized age, when Algeria and Haiti and even ancient Greece and Egypt are only a virtual visit away. Even without globalization, the writer bound to the reader, under diabolic, or even joyful, circumstances can possibly become an honorary citizen of the country of his readers.

My friend the Haitian novelist Dany Laferrière, who was a newspaper journalist during the Duvalier regime and was forced to leave for Canada during the dictatorship, has published a novel called *Je suis un écrivain japonais*, or *I Am a Japanese Writer*. In the book, the fictional author, a stand-in for Dany Laferrière, explains his decision to call himself a Japanese writer, concurring with the French literary critic Roland Barthes that "a text's unity lies not in its origin but in its destination."

"I am surprised," the fictional Laferrière writes,

to see how much attention is paid to a writer's origins. . . . I repatriated, without giving it a second thought, all the writers I read as a young man. Flaubert, Goethe, Whitman, Shakespeare, Lope de Vega, Cervantes, Kipling, Senghor, Césaire, Roumain, Amado, Diderot, they all lived in the same village that I did. Otherwise, what were they doing in my room? When, years later I myself became a writer and was asked, "Are you a Haitian writer, a Caribbean writer or a Francophone writer?" I would always answer that I took the nationality of my reader, which means that when a Japanese reader reads my books, I immediately become a Japanese writer.

Is there such a thing as an immigrant reader? he wonders.

I too sometimes wonder if in the intimate, both solitary and solidary, union between writers and readers a border can really exist. Is there a border between Antigone's desire to bury her brother and the Haitian mother of 1964 who desperately wants to take her dead son's body out of the street to give him a proper burial, knowing that if she does this she too may die? So perhaps after those executions when those young men and women were reading *Caligula*, Albert Camus became a Haitian writer. When they were reading *Oedipus Rex* and *Antigone*, Sophocles too became a Haitian writer.

"We, as we read," Ralph Waldo Emerson wrote in an essay on history, "must become Greeks, Romans, Turks, priest and king, martyr and executioner; must fasten these images to some reality in our secret experience, or we shall learn nothing rightly."

The nomad or immigrant who learns something rightly must always ponder travel and movement, just as the grief-stricken must inevitably ponder death. As does the artist who comes from a culture that is as much about harnessing life—joyous, jubilant, resilient life—as it is about avoiding death. Since he'd fashioned his dress and persona—a black suit and hat, nasal voice, and glasses—after Baron Samedi, the Vodou guardian spirit of the cemetery, François Duvalier should have known better than anyone that in Haiti people never really die. This is, after all, a place where heroes who are burned at the stake are said to evaporate into a million fireflies, where widows and widowers are advised to wear their nightgowns and pajamas inside out and wear red undergarments to keep their dead spouses out of their beds at night. And where grieving mothers are sometimes advised to wear red bras to keep their dead babies from coming back to nurse at their breasts. Like ancient Egyptians, we Haitians, when a catastrophic disaster does not prevent it, recite spells to launch our dead into the next world, all while keeping them close, building elaborate mausoleums for them in our backyards. In another country, in the cold, with no fireflies, no red underwear or backyard mausoleums, the artist immigrant, or immigrant artist, inevitably ponders the deaths that brought her here, along with the deaths that keep her here, the deaths from hunger and executions and cataclysmic devastation at home, the deaths from paralyzing chagrin in exile, and the other small, daily deaths in between.

The immigrant artist ponders death the way they did in Gabriel Garcia Márquez's Macondo, at the beginning of *One Hundred Years of Solitude.*

"We have still not had a death," Márquez's Colonel says. "A person does not belong to a place until someone is dead under the ground." And the Colonel's wife's reply might have been the same as many an immigrant artist's parents, guardian, or supporter: "If I have to die for the rest of you to stay here, then I will die."

The immigrant artist, to borrow from Toni Morrison's Nobel lecture knows what it is "to live at the edge of towns that cannot bear" our company, hamlets that need our labor but want our children banned from their schools, villages that want our sick shut out from their hospitals, big cities that want our elderly, after a lifetime of impossible labor, to pack up and go off somewhere else to die.

If I have to die for the rest of you to stay here, says the Colonel's wife, then I will die. Like her, the immigrant artist must quantify the price of the American dream in flesh and bone. All this while living with the more "regular" fears of any other artist. Do I know enough about where I've come from? Will I ever know enough about where I am? Even if somebody has died for me to stay here, will I ever truly belong?

Albert Camus once wrote that a person's creative work is nothing but a slow trek to rediscover, through the detours of art, those two or three images in whose presence his or her heart first opened. Over the years, I have tried to explore my two or three images in these rather simple essays. In each of these pieces, though, are several cities, a country, two independent republics in the same hemisphere, but obviously with different destines and goals in the world.

The immigrant artist shares with all other artists the desire to interpret and possibly remake his or her own world. So though we may not be creating as dangerously as our forebears—though we are not risking torture, beatings, execution, though exile does not threaten us into perpetual silence— still, while we are at work bodies are littering the streets somewhere. People are buried under rubble somewhere. Mass graves are being dug somewhere. Survivors are living in makeshift tent cities and refugee camps somewhere, shielding their heads from the rain, closing their eyes, covering their ears, to shut out the sounds of military "aid" helicopters. And still, many are reading, and writing, quietly, quietly.

While I was "at work" at 4:53 p.m., on January 12, 2010, the ground was shaking and killing more than two hundred thousand people in a 7.0 magnitude earthquake in Haiti. And even before the first aftershock, people were calling me asking,

"Edwidge, what are you going to do? When are you going back? Could you tell us how you feel? Could you write us fifteen hundred words or less?"

Perhaps this is why the immigrant artist needs to feel that he or she is creating dangerously even though she is not scribbling on prison walls or counting the days until a fateful date with an executioner. Or a hurricane. Or an earthquake.

Self-doubt is probably one of the stages of acclimation in a new culture. It's a staple for most artists. As immigrant artists for whom so much has been sacrificed, so many dreams have been deferred, we already doubt so much. It might have been simpler, safer to have become the more helpful doctors, lawyers, engineers our parents wanted us to be. When our worlds are literally crumbling, we tell ourselves how right they may have been, our elders, about our passive careers as distant witnesses.

Who do we think we are?

We think we are people who risked not existing at all. People who might have had a mother and father killed, either by a government or by nature, even before we were born. Some of us think we are accidents of literacy.

I do.

We think we are people who might not have been able to go to school at all, who might never have learned to read and write. We think we are the children of people who have lived in the shadows for too long. We sometimes even think that we are like the ancient Egyptians, whose gods of death demanded documentation of worthiness and acceptance before allowing them entry into the next world. Might we also be a bit like the ancient Egyptians in the way of their artists and their art, the pyramid and coffin texts, tomb paintings, and hieroglyphic makers?

One of the many ways a sculptor of ancient Egypt was described was as "one who keeps things alive." Before pictures were drawn and amulets were carved for ancient Egyptians tombs, wealthy men and women had their slaves buried with them to keep them company in the next life. The artists who came up with these other types of memorial art, the art that could replace the dead bodies, may also have wanted to save lives. In the face of both external and internal destruction, we are still trying to create as dangerously as they, as though each piece of art were a stand-in for a life, a soul, a future. As the ancient Egyptian sculptors may have suspected, and as Marcel Numa and Louis Drouin surely must have believed, we have no other choice.

Walk Straight

I am not going to make it all the way, I think. We've been walking for four hours and suddenly I have a piercing pain in my
side. My cousin Maxo's oldest son, Nick, is about thirty feet
ahead, hiking at a steady gait, following my Uncle Joseph,
who's been struggling up a steep mound on a borrowed mule.
We have been told that the mule knows the way, instinctively,
has made the journey several times before, but I haven't, not
for a while, not since I was eight years old.

Short and stout and handsome, Nick stops and pulls a pack
of menthol Comme Il Faut cigarettes out of his shirt pocket.
While lighting up, he turns around to check on me, doubled
over, hugging my midsection, where the pain has spread from
my abdomen down to my thighs. Nick walks over and puts his
nonsmoky hand on my shoulder.

"Tired?" he asks.

I want to tell him that I am more than tired, but I am saving
all my strength to ward off the pain.

"I think I'm dying," I finally manage to say.

"No you're not," he answers, chuckling before drawing once
more on his cigarette. "I was just like you when I came back

here for the first time in a while. All the walking is just catching up with your body. You'll be fine in a minute."

We stop to rest on a slick rock facing a lime-colored mountain range and take cover from the scorching midday sun under a small almond tree. Just as Nick predicted, my pain slowly subsides while he finishes his cigarette. We watch as my uncle and the mule slowly descend through a rift in the mountainside, toward our ancestral village, Beauséjour, where my paternal great-grandparents are buried and where my seventy-five-year-old Aunt Ilyana still lives.

It is the summer of 1999 and I have come to revisit these mountains from which our family has sprung and which have released us to different types of migrations. I have come to see just how far we have trekked in less than two generations, from Léogâne's rural hamlet of Beauséjour to Miami and New York City, from the valley to skyscrapers. I have come to see an aunt whom I have seen only once before in my life, when I was eight years old, because she has literally refused to come down from the mountain.

After a brief rest, I reclaim my mountain legs and continue on. Along the way, Nick and I retell each other fragmented stories about my great-grandparents—his great-great-grandparents—the furthest that memory and history go back in our family, vague tales that we've gathered from older family members. Like Tante Ilyana, both my great-grandparents lived in Beauséjour their entire lives, never venturing farther than Dabonne, the first big market town off the mountain. When they married, together they owned twenty or so acres of land and thirty pigs. Of the twelve children to whom my great-grandmother gave birth, only four made it to adulthood. My great-grandparents spent their whole lives without electricity, telephones, medical doctors, or morgues. When their children died at varying ages in childhood, they buried them the same day or the next, for lack of said morgue.

As we cross an arch of rock that forms a slanted bridge on the side of the mountain, Nick and I lament the fact that there is not more to say of our progenitors' lives beyond these indefinite segments, which could be true of almost anyone else who had lived here in these mountains.

As children, Nick and I had both come here, along with my brother Bob, to spend a week with Tante Ilyana, who is the last close family member still living in Beauséjour. Everyone else, including my grandparents, had migrated, some to the Haitian capital and others to other parts of the world. I don't remember the childhood climb up the mountain being so grueling. I remember skipping over what seemed like molehills then, compared to this endless series of cliffs and crags. I remember collecting dandelions as we passed the gardens of people who had known our fathers and grandfathers when they were our age, people who called us by the names of our aunts and uncles, people of whom there is no longer any trace. I remember plucking handfuls of vetiver and citronella, crushing them in my hand to inhale their fragrance. I don't remember the domes of bare rock. I don't remember my Aunt Ilyana's house looking so isolated from up high. I don't remember the pain in my calves, the agony of every step.

When I say this to Nick, he replies, "Perhaps it's because you were lighter, because you were a little girl."

We meet up with Uncle Joseph on the descent toward Tante Ilyana's house as he stops for a rest of his own. He offers the borrowed mule to Nick, who barely escapes a kick in the groin as he tries to mount the animal.

"This is why I have never been on one of those," I say.

"You've just never been tired enough," replies Uncle Joseph, who, at seventy-six years old, has been coming to Beauséjour from the capital a couple of times a year to visit Tante Ilyana and see after a small school that he has started here.

Uncle Joseph points out the one-room schoolhouse down below. It looks tiny and lopsided, no different from the small cemetery behind it, the cluster of marble-looking tombs where my great-grandparents are buried.

We reach Tante Ilyana's house by midafternoon. It is a modest two-room home made of limestone walls and a tin roof. The house stands between a stream and a banana grove and has not changed very much since Nick, Bob, and I came here as children, except that the tin roof has been replaced a couple of times due to rust and hurricanes. Tante Ilyana lives alone now, but her ex-husband has his own place nearby and he visits often, as does her adult son, my cousin Renel, who is a dentist in Port-au-Prince. Unlike my father, his brothers and sisters, and Renel, who followed one another to the city, Tante Ilyana remained behind with her daughter, Jeanne, until, the year before our visit, Jeanne died at the age of thirty-eight, of some unnamed deadly infectious disease passed on by her former husband. After Jeanne's death, Tante Ilyana had entombed her oldest child and only daughter in a beautiful turquoise three-tiered mausoleum next to the house. In Jeanne's mausoleum a place is reserved for Tante Ilyana, so mother and daughter can be together again in death as they had always been in life.

Tante Ilyana is not home when we arrive. Her grandsons, Jeanne's two teenage boys, who are visiting from the capital for the summer, give us some water and a large sisal mat to collapse on as we wait for her to return. We immediately crash on the front porch, in a cool spot close to the wooden railing at the other end of which the boys are pouring dried corn kernels into a grinder, turning them into bright yellow cornmeal. The boys are surrounded by twelve of Tante Ilyana's prized hens and roosters, which squawk loudly as handfuls of corn occasionally rain down on their heads.

Tante Ilyana arrives an hour or so later. She looks much younger than her seventy-five years. Her skin is an even mahogany hue and her body looks taut and lean, almost muscular. She is wearing a dark green dress and a black head wrap. She kisses Uncle Joseph and Cousin Nick hello, but, having not seen me in more than twenty-two years, does not recognize me. She lists the names of a few of my girl cousins, trying to guess who I am. Finally Uncle Joseph says, "It's Mira's daughter, Edwidge."

"Ah, Edwidge," Tante Ilyana takes my face in her firm, large hands. "Mira's daughter."

Tante Ilyana and Uncle Joseph exchange family news while Nick and I join in the corn grinding. Occasionally Tante Ilyana shouts questions to me about my parents and three brothers in New York. Has my father lost his hair? Has my mother lost weight, gained weight since my uncle showed her the last family photographs? Were any of my brothers married?

I show her a few pictures I brought for her, of my father and his receding hairline, of my plump mother, and of my three brothers, two of whom became fathers that year. With all the family news out of the way, there is nothing left to do but eat.

It is corn harvest season in the valley surrounding Tante Ilyana's house. So over the next three days, we eat lots of corn. We grill ears of corn over charcoal and firewood sticks in the thatched cooking shack by the stream. We boil them smothered with banana leaves in an aluminum pot that seems to have no bottom. We eat the sweet baby ones raw, right off the cob. From an earlier harvest, we have cornmeal paste, *mayi moulen*, for breakfast and a sweet corn flour puree, *labouyi*, for supper.

Things get going quickly that afternoon, as Uncle Joseph and Nick, who are staying nearby at the house of the school's headmistress, spend their time visiting with parents and meeting teachers, and I attach myself to Tante Ilyana.

That night over a bowl of *labouyi*, Uncle Joseph tries to convince Tante Ilyana to move to Port-au-Prince to be closer, in her old age, to him and his family.

"You're an old woman," he says. "Not that I'm wishing it, but if something happens to you, you won't be able to see a proper doctor. People die from simple illnesses here. When Jeanne died, we were barely able to arrive in time for the funeral. If you die, not that I'm wishing it, it takes so long to get here that we may not be able to see you one last time. There is no chance that your brothers in New York, Edwidge, and the others will have time to come and say good-bye. You know yourself that a corpse can last only a day or two here."

Uncle Joseph's monologue is interrupted by two shots of gunfire from somewhere in the distance. Tante Ilyana explains that it is the village chief, the *chèf seksyon*, the only legal authority in the surrounding area, signaling that he is back home from a day trip, in case anyone needs to come see him.

"Do you think life is easier for an old woman in the city?" Tante Ilyana continues. "Here I can watch over the land and over Jeanne's grave and even if you don't see me soon after I die, we'll see one another *after*."

Unlike Uncle Joseph, Tante Ilyana is not particularly religious. Every once in a while she had a *pè savann*, a lay mountain priest, come over to the cemetery to say a mass over her grandparents' graves, but only because she thought they had worked hard their whole lives and would expect it as a sign of respect. No masses were said, however, for Jeanne, who was Baptist, like my uncle.

Glancing over at Jeanne's mausoleum gleaming in the moonlight, I ask Tante Ilyana why she hadn't buried Jeanne in the cemetery near her grandparents, my great-grandparents, who, like her and Jeanne, had chosen to remain in Beauséjour.

"That cemetery belongs to a lot of people," she says. "This place is just mine and hers. When I am gone, people are going to take over the family land that is left. They already want to take it from me because I'm the only one in the family here, but this place I built for Jeanne and me is big and heavy, so maybe they will leave us alone."

The people Tante Ilyana is talking about are her few neighbors, friends and foes, who, she believes, figure that because she has so many family members in the city and abroad she doesn't need the land to live.

Changing the subject, Tante Ilyana turns to me and says, "I forgot to ask you. How is Mira's other daughter, the one who once came here as a girl? I hear that she is a *jounalis*. What was her name again, Edwidge?"

I hear a hint of pride in her voice, pride that this person, who she has momentarily forgotten is myself, has spent some time with her. A *jounalis*, or journalist, is the most common kind of writer in Haiti. A mix of usefulness—you are offering a service to others by providing information—and notoriety makes it an occasionally respectable profession, especially to someone like Tante Ilyana, who, because she was older and was needed for house and field chores, was never sent to school by her parents, and as a result does not know how to read or write. Though I am not a journalist, I know that this is her way of calling me a writer. I am overjoyed, thrilled. The separate pieces of my life have come together in that moment. I am the niece and the *jounalis*, a family writer in the eyes of my aging aunt, who has never read a word or a sentence, who has never met and will never meet another writer.

My uncle, however, raises his eyebrows in concern, as though Tante Ilyana's journalist question is proof of her increasing senility. Nick hides a smile under a cupped hand and looks at me to see how I will clarify this.

I simply and proudly say, "Tante Ilyana, I am Edwidge. I am the same one who was here."

She seems unconvinced, so I search my memory for concrete evidence of that past visit with her. Tante Ilyana and her husband were still together then, though sleeping in twin beds on opposite sides of their room, where my brother Bob, Nick, Jeanne, and I all slept on Jeanne's large sisal mat on the floor. Jeanne had been a shy but hardworking young woman. She and Tante Ilyana had spent almost every moment of their summer days together. They woke up at dawn and fetched water from the stream, made coffee for the household and everyone else who came by, sprinkled the yard with water, and swept it with sisal brooms that made a swooshing music, like a fan concert. I wandered around the yard all day, played hide and seek, lago, and hopscotch with the area girls while Nick, my brother Bob, and Tante Ilyana's husband went to work in the fields. Twice a day Tante Ilyana, Jeanne, and I would bathe in the lower end of a crystal clear stream, which was stinging cold in the morning and lukewarm in late afternoon. I was not allowed to do any work other than shell peas and sort corn kernels from the newly harvested corn because I was a city girl and the other types of work were considered too strenuous for me.

Later that night, after assigning me the twin bed where her husband used to sleep, Tante Ilyana goes out to the mausoleum to say goodnight to her daughter. "We have visitors," she tells Jeanne, part of her face shielded from the moonlight. "Mira's daughter, Edwidge, the journalist, she has come to see us again."

The next morning, I help Tante Ilyana make coffee in the cooking shed by the stream. I hold the swollen pouch, hanging from a rounded piece of coat hanger, while she pours scalding water over the coffee grounds. Uncle Joseph, Nick, and I map out the day over coffee and cassava bread with Tante Ilyana and her grandsons. There are more meetings for Nick and Uncle Joseph with a builder they had hired to add another room to the schoolhouse Uncle Joseph had paid to have built there. There are several teachers to interview for the new classes, and further curriculum planning sessions with the headmistress, a woman in her thirties who is raising three children alone, since her husband left for the Dominican Republic some years ago and never returned.

The school is Uncle Joseph's latest passion, the last thing he wants to accomplish, he says, before he dies. He has zealously collected money from family members and friends to build it so that some of the children of Beauséjour, both boys and girls, can learn to read and write.

We make our way en masse to the schoolhouse, a large open room with a dirt floor and tin roof. Tante Ilyana watches closely, narrowing her eyes, as Uncle Joseph gives special instructions to the headmistress and the builder. The headmistress puts in a plea for a blackboard for each of the new room's four walls to enable children on different levels to work independently. The schoolmistress also asks the builder to assure her of a roof that won't leak. She doesn't want to have to stop classes and send the children home whenever it rains. Tante Ilyana, who had been cooking the occasional midday meal for the children since the school first opened, volunteers herself again.

"I'll continue to do it," she says almost to herself.

I reach over and rub her shoulders, thinking, perhaps overthinking, that this is her way of making sure that other children are able to get the education that she had not.

After the schoolhouse, we walk over to the cemetery where my great-grandparents are buried. The tombs are made of cracked marble among knee-high weeds. Some of the names and dates, carved deeply on some tombstones and more superficially on others, have faded. There is no birth date for my great-grandmother Mirazine, from whom my father gets his name, Miracin, and his nickname, Mira. It is possible that her birth was never recorded at all in any public register. My great-grandmother died in 1919, during the 1915–1934 U.S. occupation of Haiti. My great-grandfather, Osnac, died after his wife did, my Tante Ilyana tells us, but the year of his death has long faded from his tombstone and her memory.

I announce that when I die, I too want to be buried in Beauséjour.

"Where would you find someone to carry you this far?" asks Tante Ilyana. "First from New York to Port-au-Prince, and then this two-day trudge up the mountains. It would be a lot of carrying."

I assure her that there would be less carrying if I were cremated and my ashes scattered from the peak of one of the mountains.

"There is already enough dust in Haiti," she says very matter-of-factly. "You should be buried where you die."

Where I die will probably not be here in this place, I think, unless the descent from the mountain proves as fatal as I had believed the climb might be.

"Enough now," says Tante Ilyana. "This is too much talk about dying."

I return a few more times to my great-grandparents' graves, often by myself. The year before, my first novel, *Breath, Eyes, Memory,* had been chosen for Oprah Winfrey's famous book club, generously exposing the book to thousands more readers than I had ever dreamed or imagined. The novel attempts to tell the story of three generations of Haitian women. Ifé Caco, the grandmother, loses her husband to a chain gain. Martine Caco, the older daughter, as a teenager is raped by a brutal Tonton Macoute whose face she never sees. Atie Caco, Martine's sister, harbors a secret love for another woman. Sophie Caco, the granddaughter, the narrator of the book, is the child who is born as a result of her mother's rape. All of these women share a trauma: all had mothers who regularly inserted the tips of their fingers into their daughters' vaginas to check that they were still virgins.

The virginity testing element of the book led to a backlash in some Haitian American circles. "You are a liar," a woman wrote to me right before I left on the trip. "You dishonor us, making us sexual and psychological misfits."

"Why was she taught to read and write?" I overheard a man saying at a Haitian American fund-raising gala in New York, where I was getting an award for writing this book. "That is not us. The things she writes, they are not us."

Maligned as we were in the media at the time, as disaster-prone refugees and boat people and AIDS carriers, many of us had become overly sensitive and were eager to censor anyone who did not project a "positive image" of Haiti and Haitians.

The letter writer was right, though. I was lying in that first book and all the other pieces of fiction I have written since. But isn't that what the word *fiction* or *novel* on the book jacket had implied? Isn't even the most elementary piece of fiction about a singularly exceptional fictional person, so that even if that fictional person is presented as an everyman or everywoman, he or she is bound to be the most exceptional everyman or everywoman fictional person of the lot? And how can one individual—be it me or anyone else—know how nine to ten million other individuals should or would behave? Furthermore, though I was not saying that "testing" happened in every Haitian household, to every Haitian girl, I knew many women and girls who had been "tested" in that way.

"You are a parasite and you exploit your culture for money and what passes for fame," is the second most common type of criticism I get from inside the community.

Anguished by my own sense of guilt, I often reply feebly that in writing what I do, I exploit no one more than myself. Besides, what is the alternative for me or anyone else who might not dare to offend? Self-censorship? Silence?

During one of my visits to my great-grandparents' grave, I had with me a book of essays titled *Afterwords: Novelists on Their Novels*, which features several writers discussing their published novels. So, while I was sitting at the gravesite, I wrote the following letter to my first novel's main character, Sophie. And since the immigrant artist must sometimes apologize for airing, or appearing to air, dirty laundry, my note to Sophie was later published as an afterword in all subsequent editions of the book, becoming an addendum to the text.

Dear Sophie,

I am writing you this note while sitting on the edge of my great-grandmother's grave, an elevated tombstone in the high mountains of Léogâne, overlooking a majestic lime-colored mountain range. Suspended as I am here, far from terra firma and close to the clouds, I feel that this is the only place in the world where I truly belong. This is the place that I most wished as a home for you too, the place I had in mind when I had Tante Atie stand with you in the middle of a cemetery plot and pronounce, "Walk straight, you are in the presence of family."

I guess I have always felt, writing about you, that I was in the presence of family, a family full of kindness as well as harshness, a family full of love as well as grief, a family deeply rooted in the past yet struggling to confront an unpredictable future. I felt blessed to have encountered this family of yours, the Cacos, named after a bird whose wings look like flames. I feel blessed to have shared your secrets, your mother's, your aunt's, your grandmother's secrets, mysteries deeply embedded in you, in them, much like the wiry vetiver clinging to the side of these hills.

I write this to you now, Sophie, because your secrets, like you, like me, have traveled far from this place. Your experiences in the night, your grandmother's obsessions, your mother's "tests" have taken on a larger meaning and your body is now being asked to represent a larger space than your flesh. You are being asked, I have been told, to represent every girl child, every woman from this land that you and I love so much. Tired of protesting, I feel I must explain. Of course, not all Haitian mothers are like your mother. Not all Haitian daughters are tested as you have been.

I have always taken for granted that this story, which is yours, and only yours, would always be read as such. But some of the voices that come back to me, to you, to these hills respond with a different kind of understanding than I had hoped. And so I write this to you now, Sophie, as I write it to myself, praying that the singularity of your experience be allowed to exist, along with your own peculiarities, inconsistencies, your own voice. And I write this note to you, thanking you for the journey of healing— from here and back—that you and I have been through together, with every step wishing that both our living and our dead will rest in peace.

May these words bring wings to your feet,
Edwidge Danticat
Summer 1999

Our last two days in Beauséjour proceed like most reunions, with the awe of reconnecting with a loved one slowly being replaced by daily routine. Uncle Joseph and Nick lose themselves in the details of the school while Tante Ilyana and I talk less and less, to avoid, I suspect, speaking of separation. There are already so many separations in our family, constant departures and returns. We cannot afford to curse or avoid these exits and migrations, however, because they have earned us whatever type of advancement we have made. Tante Ilyana's son Renel, for example, had to spend most of his life away from her in order to become a dentist, while her daughter Jeanne, who stayed behind with her, died an agonizing and prolonged death, showing Tante Ilyana that some departures are inevitable, which is why Jeanne's children now live in the capital with their father's relatives and visit Beauséjour only in the summer.

The night before we are to leave, I am lying on my back in the bed where Tante Ilyana's husband used to sleep, listening to her chatter in her sleep. Mid-dream, she laughs and makes promises. "Listen," she says. "Come back soon. I'll send you coffee."

In the dark, I imagine that from here she can talk to all of us across these long distances, to my father, her parents, my brothers, and their children. And while I am making this silent invocation, Tante Ilyana awakens herself from yet another dream and whispers from across the room, "Edwidge, are you sleeping?

I say, "No. But it is not you who is keeping me awake."

It is the mountains maybe, it being so quiet here at night that you hear everything, the swing of every tree branch, the bubbling of the stream, the footsteps of night travelers and wandering animals. And I listen for everything because I know it won't always be so. I listen too closely and sometimes the listening gets too loud.

The next morning as we are preparing to leave, Tante Ilyana presents me with a three-pound sack of coffee beans to bring to my father in Brooklyn.

"When he has a taste of this coffee," she says, "it will bring him home."

I marvel at the magic of this coffee of which Tante Ilyana is so certain. What if such a thing did exist, an elixir against fading memories, a panacea to evoke images of spaces lost to us, to instantly return us home. I thank Tante Ilyana for the coffee on my father's behalf by telling her a story, something I knew about him and she didn't. I tell her of going with my father to a Chinese herbalist in New York who was treating him for psoriasis and of the Chinese herbalist telling my father to stop drinking coffee or he would never be cured. And of my father saying, "Doctor, there must be another way," because he would never give up coffee. And in one of those strange crossed-wire moments, my story gives Tante Ilyana pause, and she says that perhaps she shouldn't send the coffee to my father if it means that he'd have psoriasis forever. I must convince her to give me the coffee again, and finally she does.

The next morning at five a.m., we start out, Uncle Joseph, Nick, and I, for our journey down the mountain. Our plan is to be halfway down by eleven a.m., before the sun gets too high in the sky, making it too hot to walk without fainting. We will stop briefly for lunch at the house of a friend of my uncle's and then hike the rest of the afternoon, which would mean that we'd be in Port-au-Prince around seven or eight in the evening.

The trip up took us two days, but Nick and Uncle Joseph assure me that it will be faster going down since we are not stopping for the night. Besides, with gravity it is always easier to descend than to climb, even with a three-pound sack of coffee in my backpack.

My way of saying good-bye is always the same. I pretend that later in the day or the next day or the day after I will see the person to whom I am bidding farewell. It is the only way I can endure separations, large and small, without becoming totally incapacitated with sadness. Tante Ilyana's way is more abrupt and formal and perhaps healthier. We kiss each other on the cheek as she lists the names of all the family members in New York to whom I should give her regards. She and Jeanne's boys walk with us for a mile or so and then they stop walking and we continue on.

The journey down is, as my cousin and uncle predicted, much easier. Rather than walk in a straight line, I zigzag through the difficult roads, forming invisible Zs with my feet all over the mountain roads, which is, my uncle tells me, the way the peasants climb and descend these mountains with relative ease. This is why they don't look as tired and burdened as I do when I finally reach Dabonne and climb with great relief into my cousin's open-backed truck. That and the fact that they are used to it, my uncle says. "If you did this often enough you too would get used to it."

I begin to worry about Tante Ilyana on the car ride back to the capital, imposing on her life visions of extreme comforts that are lacking even in mine. I imagine her having her own helicopter in which to travel to and from the market. I think of her bypassing the stream baths for a Jacuzzi. I see her on vacation, visiting the Statue of Liberty, Disney World, the Empire State Building, the Eiffel Tower. By some standards, she's seen little of the world, but perhaps, I tell myself, her world is larger than all of these places. I remind myself that at least she has a simple life, which I have at different times attempted to replicate in arbitrary ways, by not buying too many clothes, too much furniture. At the same time, Tante Ilyana's life seems far from simple. Her vocation is nothing less than to maintain our family's physical legacy, to guard a very small house in the ancestral village, to sustain a faraway world to which we could return, if we wanted to, and find traces, however remote and faint, of who we are.

When I find out a year later that Tante Ilyana is dead, I am at my parents' house babysitting my sixteen-month-old nephew Ezekiel, who had recently learned to run. It is no longer easy to keep Ezekiel still on my lap during serious conversations, as he wants to use his newly discovered mobility as much as possible: by skipping from spot to spot, from my father's knees to mine, from the living room sofa to the window curtains to the television set, which, with his safety in mind, we have placed on the floor rather than on a teetering table. Ezekiel is also exercising his newly discovered oral abilities by shouting nonsensical words, and my father must compete with him as he says, "I had a call from Haiti just now and they told me Ilyana died."

The grief on my father's face is clouded with logistical figurations. It had taken a whole day for news of the death to travel to Port-au-Prince and then by telephone to us, which means that Tante Ilyana's funeral has already taken place. Attending is not even an option.

Ezekiel shrieks with pride when he finally succeeds in turning on the television set by himself, and I'm grateful for the distraction, for having to run and save him from discoveries for which I fear he's not ready.

Ezekiel squirms as I hold him in my lap and try to quiet him down, and I find in my efforts to keep him still—whispering his name in his ear, promising him sweets he'd never get, singing the alphabet song he loves so much—that he is the one who is momentarily saving my father and me from our sadness.

There is little to say, or neither my father nor I can find the words, so I offer a confession instead. This revelation also seems to interest young Ezekiel as he watches my trembling lips.

I tell my father that on the last day of my visit to Beauséjour, Tante Ilyana had given me three pounds of coffee for him, coffee that had been confiscated as "illegal agricultural transport" by customs officers at John F. Kennedy Airport in New York. I hadn't told him about the coffee previously for fear that he would needlessly mourn something that in the end he'd never have. There is perhaps more I want to confess, but I know these disclosures will also not help with his sorrow or mine. I should have stayed much longer in Beauséjour, spoken more to Tante Ilyana. I should have pretended I was the journalist she believed me to be, asked her many more questions about the family, about herself. I shouldn't have seen the visit as routine, as my uncle and cousin, who were then living in Haiti, had. I should have foreseen that it might be the last time I'd see Tante Ilyana. After all, she was old and far away. But all these regrets might have been as painful to ponder then in the mountains as they are now.

"You should have told me about the coffee," my father says, while reaching over and rescuing Ezekiel from my tight grasp. "We sure need that coffee now."

We certainly could have used it that day, Tante Ilyana's magic elixir, to help us remember and forget.

After managing to hold Ezekiel still for a while, my father puts him back on the floor. Ezekiel runs from us and immediately returns to the TV set, which he turns on again with glee. He stands there and stares in awe at the eye-level faces on the screen, and then trots over to touch them. He seems heartbroken to discover that the people are flat and cannot respond to him. Then he steps back and walks to my father, grabbing his knee and burying his face in his pant leg.

As my father strokes young Ezekiel's head, consoling his brief frustration, I realize that my way of saying good-bye, at least to Tante Ilyana, would never again be the same. I could no longer pretend that later in the day, or the next day, or even the following year I would ever see her or hear her call me a *jounalis* again.

I Am Not a Journalist

I began writing this essay on Monday, April 3, 2000, the morning that one of Haiti's most famous journalists, the radio commentator Jean Dominique, was assassinated. That morning, I awakened to a series of alarming phone calls, the first simply reporting a rumor that Jean might have been shot while arriving at his radio station, Radio Haiti Inter, at six-thirty that morning for the daily news and editorial program he coanchored with his wife, Michèle Montas. The next few callers declared for certain that Jean had been shot: seven bullets in the head, neck, and chest. The final morning calls finally confirmed that Jean was dead.

The following hours would slip by in a haze as I went to teach my classes at the University of Miami, where I was a visiting professor that spring. When I came back to my office that afternoon, there were still more phone calls and e-mails from relatives, friends, and acquaintances, who could not believe what had happened. In those real and virtual conversations, the phrase that emerged most often was "Not Jean Do!"

During the varying lengths of time that many of us had known Jean Dominique—either as a voice on Haitian radio or in person—we had all come to think of him as heroically invincible. After all, he had survived the Duvalier dictatorship, during which his older brother Philippe had been murdered while participating in yet another failed invasion attempt to topple François Duvalier by taking over the military barracks across the street from Duvalier's residence at the national palace.

Unlike his brother, Jean had survived several arrests and their resulting exiles, and had lived to return to Haiti to open and reopen his radio station, where being the owner and director allowed him a kind of autonomy that few hired journalists could manage in a volatile political climate. Jean had expressed his opinions freely, seemingly without fear, criticizing groups as well as individuals, organizations, and institutions who'd proven themselves to be inhumane, unethical, or simply unjust. Of course, Jean's life was too multifaceted and complex to fully grasp and make sense of in these very early hours so soon after his death. What seemed undeniably compelling and memorable about him at that moment was his exceptional passion for Haiti and how that passion had finally betrayed him.

I couldn't sort out fully, under this full assault of memories, the exact moment when I had met Jean Dominique. As a child in Haiti, I had heard his voice on the radio many times, sometimes blaring from ours or neighboring houses at the highest possible volume. As an adult in New York, I had seen him at so many different Haiti-related gatherings that I can't even pinpoint our first in-person meeting. I do, however, remember the first time we had a lengthy conversation. It was at an art exhibit at Ramapo College in 1994. The exhibit was curated by our mutual friend, the filmmaker Jonathan Demme, and featured three emerging Haitian artists. The night of the exhibit,

Jean was in exile yet again, after some U.S.-trained colonels leading the Haitian military had deposed President Jean-Bertrand Aristide and had raided and destroyed Jean's radio station. The night of the art exhibit, Jean and I talked at length about the strikingly colorful paintings on display and the extreme nostalgia that they evoked in him, the hunger to return to his home and his radio station in Haiti as soon as he could.

A few weeks later, Jonathan Demme asked Jean and me to work with him on a project about the history of Haitian cinema. Every week, the three of us would meet on the Ramapo College campus to discuss Haitian cinema while some communications students watched and videotaped us. I said very little at those sessions, feeling rather shy sitting between two obsessive cinephiles. My job was to find prints of the films that we could discuss. Jean's was to help us all understand them by putting them in context as Jonathan questioned him about technique, content, and style.

During the dictatorship, in the early 1960s, a young Jean had created a cinema club, hosting weekly screenings at the Alliance Française in Port-au-Prince. There he showed films such as Federico Fellini's *La Strada*, which is, among other things, about a girl's near enslavement as a circus performer.

"If you see a good film correctly," Jean said, "the grammar of that film is a political act. Every time you see Fellini's *La Strada*, even if there is no question of fascism, of political persecution, you feel something against the black part of life."

Another favorite of his was the Alain Resnais documentary *Night and Fog*, which describes the horrors of concentration camps. "To us, Auschwitz was Fort Dimanche," he said, referring to the Duvalier-era dungeonlike prison where thousands of Haitians were tortured and killed.

In 1964, the year Marcel Numa and Louis Drouin were executed, the Ciné Club was shut down by the Haitian military after a screening of *Night and Fog* at the Alliance Française. Jean then briefly turned to filmmaking, codirecting and narrating a short tongue-in-cheek documentary, *Mais je suis belle* (But I Am Beautiful), about a Haitian beauty pageant. This was, it is said, one of the first films made by Haitians in Haiti.

The task of finding the prints for the Haitian films being discussed in our Ramapo History of Haitian Cinema class proved herculean, as many of the filmmakers, including Jean, had lost track of their own prints during nomadic lives in exile. In our videotaped sessions, however, each time we'd mention a film title to Jean, he would proceed to describe at length not only the plot of the film but also extensive details of the method of its distribution and the political framework surrounding it. The film *Anita*, for example, made by Jean's contemporary Rassoul Labuchin, told the story of a servant girl who is abused by the city relative to whom she'd been given by her peasant parents.

According to Labuchin, during the Ciné Club days, Jean had held conferences for aspiring filmmakers, encouraging them to view the seventh art as being essential to the majority of Haitians, particularly those who could not read. The most recent studies suggest that only about 56 percent of Haitians are literate. The actual figure is probably lower than that if one defines literate as, for example, being able to read an entire book. Perhaps this is why the visual arts have flourished in Haiti. Painters do not necessarily need to know how to read or write. This is what Jean had hoped filmmakers would do with film—make it, like radio and painting, a medium that would be not only open and available but also welcoming to those who were shut off from other means of information, communication and entertainment. "Jean asked us to develop screenplays," Labuchin would later say, "that meant something to the Haitian people."

During our Haitian cinema class, Jean told us how he and Labuchin had traveled together with Labuchin's film, *Anita*, screening it throughout the Haitian countryside to discourage peasants from giving their children away to better-off families in the city. The film, which begins as a harshly realistic treatise on the *restavèk* child labor system in Haiti, ends as a musical fantasy in which the child servant is consoled by a fairy godmother played by the brilliant Haitian-German singer, Cornelia Shutt, better known as Ti Corn.

In the same vein, Jean had also broadcast on his radio station the Creole soundtrack of a film based on the classic Haitian novel *Gouverneurs de la rosée* (Masters of the Dew), written by the Haitian novelist Jacques Roumain and later translated into English by the poet Langston Hughes and scholar Mercer Cook. In Manuel—Roumain's Sophoclean hero—and his peasant family and friends, Jean saw prototypes of poor Haitians, who were either condemned to a desperate life or driven to migrate, only to return to Haiti to face the impossibility of reintegration or even death. Jean was extremely proud of having aired the Creole teleplay of the novel on his radio station because whenever he visited the countryside, the peasants would tell him how they had recognized themselves and their lives in the words of Roumain's book.

Masters of the Dew begins with Délira Délivrance, Manuel's old peasant mother, plunging her hands into the dust and declaring, "We're all going to die. Animals, plants, every living soul!" Délira's despair turns into hope when her son returns from the sugarcane fields of Cuba, greeting every living thing he encounters on his way to his parents' house by singing, "Growing things, growing things! To you I say, 'Honor!' You must answer 'Respect,' so that I may enter. You are my house, you're my country."

Délira's despair and Manuel's hope make for a delicate balance, of which I am reminded each time I return to Haiti: the exile's joy and the resident's anguish—it can also be the other way around, the resident's joy and the exile's anguish—clashing.

While in exile in New York in the early 1990s, at the insistence of some friends, Jean would occasionally participate in a television or radio program dealing with the injustices of the military regime in Haiti, which by then had killed almost eight thousand people, including a well-known businessman named Antoine Izméry and the then justice minister, Guy Malary. Since Jean had known both Izméry and Malary, after their deaths he agreed to appear as a guest panelist on *The Charlie Rose Show* and was seated in the audience at a taping of the *Phil Donahue Show* when the subject was Haiti. During the Donahue taping, Jean squirmed in his seat while Phil Donahue held up the stubbed elbow of Alèrte Bélance, a woman who had been attacked with machetes by members of the junta's paramilitary branch, who cut off her tongue and arm. After the taping, Jean seemed almost on the verge of tears as he said, "My country needs hope."

Our Haitian cinema project came to an end at the close of the semester. After that, Jonathan, Jean, and I would occasionally meet in Jonathan's office in Nyack, New York, for further discussions.

One day, while driving to Nyack with Jonathan's assistant producer, Neda, Jean told us about a word he'd rediscovered in a Pedro Almodóvar film he had seen the night before: *guapa*! While puffing on his ever-present pipe, Jean took great pains to explain to us that someone who was *guapa* was extremely beautiful and courageous—courageously beautiful, he added. Demanding further clarification, Neda and I would take turns shouting out the names of women that the three of us knew, starting with Michèle, Jean's wife.

"Michèle is very . . . "

"*Guapa!*" he yelled back with great enthusiasm. This was one of the many times that Jean's vibrant love of life, and his total devotion to his wife, Michèle, shone forth.

On that *guapa* day, Neda had to stay in Nyack, so she gave me the car and told me to drive Jean back to Manhattan. I refrained from telling her that even though I'd had my license for three years, I had never driven any car but the one owned by the driving school where I'd learned. When I confessed this to Jean, he wisely offered to drive. We drove for hours through New York's Rockland County and the Palisades, and then over the George Washington Bridge, finally realizing we were completely lost, with Jean trying to smoke a pipe and follow my uncertain directions at the same time.

When we finally got to Manhattan late in the afternoon and Jean turned the car over to me, he seemed worried as I pulled away from the curb, and watched until I turned the corner, blending into Manhattan traffic.

The democratically elected president, Jean-Bertrand Aristide, was restored to power soon after that day. The next time I would see Jean would be at his and Michèle's house in Haiti.

"Jean, you're looking *guapa*," I told him.

He laughed.

It was wonderful to see Jean move about within his own walls, surrounded by his own books, pictures and paintings, knowing that he had been dreaming about coming back home almost every minute he was in exile.

Later at dinner, Jean spoke mournfully about those who'd died during and after the coup d'état: Antoine Izméry, Guy Malary, and later a well-loved priest, Father Jean-Marie Vincent. Adding Jean's name now to those of these very public martyrs still seems unimaginable, given how passionately he expressed his hope that such assassinations would stop taking place.

"It has to stop," I remember him saying. "It has to stop."

The plane that took me from Miami to Haiti the day before Jean's funeral seemed like a microcosm of Haiti. Crammed on a 727 for an hour and thirty minutes were young, well-to-do college students returning from Miami-area campuses for the weekend, vendors traveling with suitcases filled with merchandise from abroad, three male deportees being expatriated from the United States, a cluster of older women in black, perhaps also returning for a funeral, and, up front, the former president of Haiti, Jean-Bertrand Aristide, returning from a speaking engagement at the University of Miami Law School. That we were all on this plane, listening to flight announcements in French, English, and Creole, seemed somewhat unreal. I couldn't help but recall one of the many conversations that Jean and I had while lost in the Palisades in New York that afternoon.

I had told him that I envied the certainty with which he could and often did say the words, "My country." "My country is suffering," he would say. "It's being held captive by criminals. My country is slowly dying, melting away."

"My country, Jean," I said, "is one of uncertainty. When I say 'my country' to some Haitians, they think I mean the United States. When I say 'my country' to some Americans, they think of Haiti."

My country, I felt, both as an immigrant and as an artist, was something that was then being called the tenth department. Haiti then had nine geographic departments and the tenth was the floating homeland, the ideological one, which joined all Haitians living outside of Haiti, in the *dyaspora*.

I meant, in the essay that I began to write the morning that Jean died, to struggle to explain the multilayered meaning of the Creole word *dyaspora*. I meant to borrow a phrase from a speech given by the writer Gérard Alphonse-Férère at the Haitian Embassy in Washington, DC, on August 27, 1999, in which he describes diaspora/*dyaspora* as a "term employed to refer to any dispersal of people to foreign soils." But in the Haitian context it is used "to identify the hundreds of thousands of Haitians living in many countries of the world." I meant in that essay to list my own personal experiences as an immigrant and a writer, of being called *dyaspora* when expressing an opposing political point of view in discussions with friends and family members living in Haiti, who knew that they could easily silence me by saying, "What do you know? You're living outside. You're a *dyaspora*." I meant to recall some lighter experiences of being startled in the Haitian capital or in the provinces when a stranger who wanted to catch my attention would call out, "*Dyaspora!*" as though it were a title like *Miss, Ms., Mademoiselle,* or *Madame.* I meant to recall conversations or debates in restaurants, at parties, or at public gatherings where members of the *dyaspora* would be classified—justifiably or not—as arrogant, insensitive, overbearing, and pretentious people who were eager to reap the benefits of good jobs and political positions in times of stability in a country that they'd fled and stayed away from during difficult times. Shamefacedly, I'd bow my head and accept these judgments when they were expressed, feeling guilty about my own physical distance from a country I had left at the age of twelve during a dictatorship that had forced thousands to choose between exile or death.

In this essay, however, I can't help but think of Jean's reaction to my, in retrospect, inconsequential *dyaspora* dilemma, in a conversation we had when I visited his radio station to discuss a Creole program that Jonathan had created from one of my Haiti-based short stories, a radio play about a man who steals a hot air balloon to fly away from Haiti. Translating—retranslating—that story from the original English in which I had written it had been a surreal experience. It was as if the voice in which I write, the voice in which people speak Creole that comes out English on paper, had been released and finally I was writing for people like my Tante Ilyana, people who did not read, not because they did not have enough time or because they had too many other gadgets and distractions, but because they had never learned how.

Now I am suddenly back in the old essay, back to bowing my head in shame at being called a parasitic *dyaspora,* a foreign being but still not a *blan*, and I want to bring the old essay into this one with these words from Jean: "The *Dyaspora* are people with their feet planted in both worlds," he said. "There's no need to be ashamed of that. There are more than a million of you. You all are not alone."

Having been exiled many times himself to that very *dyaspora* that I was asking him to help me define, Jean could commiserate with all of us exiles, émigrés, refugees, migrants, nomads, immigrants, naturalized citizens, half-generation, first-generation, American, Haitian, Haitian American, men, women, and children who were living in the United States and elsewhere. Migration in general was something he understood well, whether from the countryside—what many in Haiti called the *peyi andeyò*, the outside country—to the Haitian capital, or from Haitian borders to other shores.

Jean's funeral was held at the Sylvio Cator soccer stadium in downtown Port-au-Prince, where thousands streamed by his coffin and the coffin of Jean Claude Louissaint, a watchman at the radio station who was gunned down in the radio station's parking lot along with Jean. T-shirts with Jean's face had been distributed and everyone, including his wife, daughters, and sisters, wore them at the stadium that day. Banners demanding justice for the murders lined many Port-au-Prince streets and graffiti expressing similar sentiments covered the walls of government buildings. At the stadium ceremony, Jean received a posthumous service medal from the Haitian government. But his real funeral was held a week later in the Artibonite Valley, where as a young man he had worked as an agronomist. There his ashes were scattered in Haiti's largest river, at the heart of the country's breadbasket. The ashes were scattered by his wife, Michèle, along with several peasant organization leaders he had befriended over the years.

In her memoir, *Mémoire errante*, Jan J. Dominique, the novelist and radio personality who is Jean Dominique's daughter and phonetic namesake, writes of the Artibonite Valley ceremony that during Jean's wake she witnessed the creation of a myth when someone told Jean's wife, Michèle, "You know, Madame Jean, he often came to see us. He would follow us across the river all the way to the coffee plantations high in the mountains. He would sleep with us, share in our way of life. He was just here, a month ago."

"Michèle looked over at me," noted Jan J. "I am bewildered. My father has never lived, in recent years, in this region. He had not left Port-au-Prince last month. When he went to the Artibonite it was to work as a journalist and activist. He neither planted nor harvested in the fields. We do not correct this man. We had not yet even scattered my father's ashes in the river when he had already become a legend."

I remember watching footage of the scattering of Jean's ashes, which were passed in a corn-husk-covered calabash from his wife's trembling hands to that of several local farmers before they were emptied into the slow-moving water. I remember thinking how ample they were, these bountiful ashes, for such a skinny man.

The footage of the scattering of the ashes is now part of a documentary that Jonathan Demme was directing about Jean's life. The documentary would be titled *The Agronomist* because, during one of the many interviews that Jonathan conducted with Jean—when Jonathan had envisioned a film that would end with Jean's triumphant return from exile—Jean, who is often referred to as Haiti's most famous journalist, told Jonathan, "You will be surprised, but I am not a journalist. I am an agronomist."

Jean had been dead for eight months, and the Haitian government's investigation into his death had been going nowhere, when I met his widow, Michèle Montas, in a Manhattan restaurant in December 2000 to interview her for an article I was writing about the case for *The Nation* magazine. Michèle was indeed *guapa*, a tall, striking, usually cheerful woman, but the day we met to talk about Jean's death in detail for the first time, she was looking just as sad as she had at his funeral months earlier. At lunch, she barely sipped her water. When the waiter came to check on her glass, he stopped to ask about a button pinned to her jacket. On the button was a picture of Jean. Above Jean's piercing eyes, raised eyebrows, and high forehead were the words *Jean Dominique vivan* (Jean Dominique Lives).

"Who is Jean Dominique?" the waiter asked Michèle.

"My husband," she said.

For more than two decades, excluding stretches of time when they were twice forced into exile, the two had worked together, coanchoring a morning news program, the highlights of which were Dominique's commentaries on Haitian social and political life. Friends and foes listened to them, to "smell the air and test the waters," as Jean liked to say, "get closer to the *beton*," gauge the mood of the streets. Had it been any other morning, Jean and Michèle would have been together when he and Jean Claude Louissaint were assassinated in the radio station's parking lot.

"We usually drove to work together," Michèle explained, carefully drawing out her words, as though to pace herself so she would not cry. "That morning, Jean left ten minutes before me to look at some international news for the program. As I got in the car, leaving home, I heard some usual announcements on the radio and then silence. I called the station and the person who answered told me, 'Just come!' When I pulled into the parking lot, the police were there. I saw Jean Claude Louissaint, and then I saw Jean's body on the ground. I called to him, but he didn't answer. I rushed upstairs to call the doctor, thinking something could be done. I didn't believe he was dead until the doctor confirmed it."

Even though the then outgoing president, René Préval, was a close friend of Jean and Michèle, eight months later the murder remained unsolved. In the final state of the nation address of his first term, President Préval admitted that the biggest weakness of his five-year presidency had been justice. Citing Jean's case, he warned his parliamentarians, "If we leave this corpse at the crossroads of impunity, we should watch out so that the same people who killed Jean do not kill us as well."

That fall, an important lead in the case had vanished when a suspect, Jean Wilner Lalanne, was shot as he was being arrested. The thirty-two-year-old Lalanne later died, reportedly of respiratory complications and cardiac arrest, during surgery meant to remove three bullets from his buttocks. Lalanne's body then disappeared from the morgue and has never been found.

A month after Dominique's death, on May 3, 2000, Michèle reopened Radio Haiti Inter, starting her first solo broadcast with her habitual greeting to her husband, "Bonjour, Jean." I was there in the studio the morning the station reopened, with Jonathan Demme and many other friends of Jean and Michèle. President Préval was there as well. Aside from filming and milling around, there was very little else we could do. Our presence was the worst kind of comfort. We were all there, crowding hallways, giving hugs, taking notes, being generally underfoot, because Jean was not. In a poignant and poetic editorial the morning the radio reopened, Michèle announced to her listeners that "Jean Léopold Dominique, independent journalist, is not dead. He is with us in our studios." She went on to detail what the button could not, that those who tried so violently to silence Jean could never really succeed. Like Prometheus, she said, he'd learned how to steal fire from the gods.

Her broadcast was followed by three days of old Dominique programs, ranging from a lengthy interview with a woman whose child, like sixty other Haitian children, had died after taking toxic Chinese cough medication distributed by a Haitian pharmaceutical company, to a peasant leader contesting a fertilizer price hike, to conversations with Haitian playwrights and filmmakers.

During the months that followed Jean's assassination, Michèle often had the impossible task of reporting on the air about the investigation into his death. Though Haitian law bound her to secrecy as a party in the investigation, she was not prevented from commenting on aspects of the inquest that were in the public record.

"Every time I feel that the investigation is slowing down," she told me at lunch, "I realize I must say something. I have to ask the judge's permission to do it, but if there is something I feel that people must know, I have to report it. What I am try-ing to do is get it to the point of no return, where things must be resolved. Rather than reporting the story, we became part of the story. There are times when you cannot stay out of the story even if you want to."

During the eight months following Jean's death, Michèle participated in rallies and demonstrations, picketing along with other journalists, victims' rights groups, and peasant organizations, demanding that Jean's killers be found and prosecuted.

"This corpse will not lie cold," she said. "The issue of Jean's death has taken a large place in the country. People are asking for justice for Jean but also for protection. People feel that if my husband can be killed, then others can be, too. We need to end this climate of impunity and find justice now."

Perhaps more than anyone else in Haiti in those days, Michèle knew how difficult that task might be. She worried, as time passed, that her husband's name would be added to the long list of nearly forgotten martyrs, some of whose faces loomed from posters lining the hallway of their radio station.

"A lot of what I have been trying to do is keep Jean alive," she said. "It's an important thing for me right now. Fifty percent of my energy goes toward that."

Who does she think killed Jean, I ask.

"I don't know," she says. "After all, I am a journalist. I cannot deal in rumors. I am looking for facts, for proof. The most im-portant step to resolution is knowing the truth. All I know is, the fact that we don't know who paid for this crime puts us all in danger."

Michèle was somewhat encouraged when a police officer was arrested after he was found in possession of a car that had been identified as having been at the crime scene.

"I feel that something is moving," she said at that time. "We are approaching something. We are getting closer to more apparent leads."

The leads never materialized, however. One suspect, a senator, refused to cooperate with the investigation, claiming parliamentary immunity. The investigating judges fled the country, fearing for their lives. On Christmas Day 2002, a potential assassin walked into Michèle's yard in a suburb of Port-au-Prince and began shooting, killing Maxime Seide, one of her young bodyguards. The assassin had come to kill her, but had been scared away by Maxime Seide's heroic intervention.

I was in Haiti then with my husband, spending Christmas with my mother-in-law in a small southern town. We were listening to the radio that my mother-in-law always had on in the house when we heard a news bulletin falsely stating that Michèle had been killed. We managed to clear things up by calling some mutual friends who assured us that Michèle was very much alive. I could not fully believe it, however, until I saw her again.

When my husband and I saw her at her house shortly after the assassination attempt, she was calm but sorrowful. She had escaped death again, yet someone had died in her place. She was at times angry and defiant, but already one could tell that it was all beginning to weigh on her, the responsibility for herself, for her elderly mother—who had been with her during the assassination attempt—and the journalists and others who worked at the radio station and were getting more and more threats as yet another inconclusive report on Jean's assassination was made public.

In March 2003, as the threats continued, Michèle Montas closed the radio station to which she and her husband had given several decades of their lives, and moved back to New York. This was her first solo exile since she and Jean had been together.

"We have lost three lives in three years," Michèle told an American journalist shortly after pulling Radio Haiti Inter off the air. "I was no longer willing to go to another funeral."

CHAPTER 4

Daughters of Memory

I first read Jan J. Dominique, the Haitian novelist and daughter of Jean Dominique, when I could still read an entire book in French without once consulting a dictionary. Five years before, at age twelve, I had left Haiti (where I had been living with my uncle and aunt) and had moved to Brooklyn, New York, to be reunited with my parents. Being new to a place where schoolmates felt free to call me a dirty Haitian or Frenchie or boat person, I hungered for words from home. Reading in New York would not be like reading back in Haiti, where rote memorization was the primary method of learning for children my age and where I had memorized, then recited, and then quickly forgotten at least a million unsavored words. If anything, I had resented those forgotten words, their length and complication, their impenetrability, their occasional irrelevance to my tropical reality. We had been made to memorize, for example, lessons about seasons, which listed them as *le printemps, l'été, l'automne, et l'hiver*—spring, summer, fall, and winter—without acknowledging the dry or rainy seasons, or even the hurricane seasons, around us. At least we were not obliged to recite the French colonial creed, "Our ancestors the

Gauls" with our African lips while staring ahead from our black faces with our dark eyes. But there were still some necessary erasures, one of them being the fact that, because of the dictatorship and its brutal censorship, I knew no child who had read even a short novel by a Haitian-born writer. What we got in school were excerpts from certain French novels, among them *Camille* and *The Three Musketeers* by Alexandre Dumas père et fils, who had a Haitian grandmother and great-grandmother in Marie-Cesette Dumas.

Many older students also read the meticulous details of Émile Zola's downtrodden classes, which strongly echoed some of the realties of my own impoverished neighborhood. These and the fables of La Fontaine, the pensées of Blaise Pascal, and the crude jokes of François Rabelais filled whatever space and time might have been devoted to homegrown contemporary talent. I can hear now as I write this cries of protest from other Haitians my age (and younger and older, too) shouting from the space above my shoulders, the bleachers above every writer's shoulders where readers cheer or hiss and boo in advance. They are hissing now, that chorus or a portion of it, decrying this as both a contradiction and a lie. "I read Haitian writers when I was twelve," they say, but I must stop and turn to them now and say, I am speaking only for myself.

One of my young literature teachers in primary school, Miss Roy, loved French literature so much that she was always quoting from it. "*Comme a dit l'auteur*," or "As the writer said," she would begin, before citing Voltaire, Racine, Baudelaire—writers to whose words we must be exposed, she thought, in order to be fully "civilized."

I would later become a French literature major in college, I think because I secretly worshipped her. I remember her cocoa brown skin, her manicured nails, and her forced Parisian accent, her slight hint of vetiver perfume, her perfectly creased clothes, her face that never sweated, even on the hottest days, when in the heat's haze it would appear almost as though her spiky high heel shoes were not even touching the ground. If my angelic literature teacher knew the existence of home-grown literature, she never betrayed the fact.

So I first read Jan J. Dominique when I could still read an entire book in French without consulting a dictionary. At seventeen, after having lived in the United States for five years, I went on what had become a regular weekly quest for reading material at the main branch of the Brooklyn Public Library one Saturday afternoon and was shocked to come across two new narrow shelves of books labeled *Livres Haitiens*, or Haitian books, most of them still crisp and new as though they had each been carefully packaged and lovingly hand-delivered to those shelves. The thirty-year Duvalier dictatorship had just ended in Haiti, and perhaps some of the more vocal Haitian patrons of the Brooklyn library had demanded more books about themselves to help them interpret their ever-changing country from afar.

I checked out the only two novels remaining among the poetry collections and political essays: Jan J. Dominique's *Mémoire d'une amnésique* (Memoir of an Amnesiac), and the French edition of Jacques Roumain's *Gouverneurs de la rosée*, (Masters of the Dew). Because the Roumain book was shorter, I devoured it first, and perhaps it is thanks to that eager first reading that I have tried to maintain a silent conversation with Jacques Roumain that publicly manifested itself in the title of my 2004 book *The Dew Breaker*, a book that I intended to be neither a novel nor a story collection, but something in between. The longing to converse with Roumain is not mine alone. In a tribute on the hundredth anniversary of his birth, Jan J. Dominique wrote, "Over the years, Jacques Roumain has often been present in my life. For various reasons ranging from literature to politics, to Vodou, to linguistics choices, to personal considerations and professional activities. Roumain has sometimes infiltrated my daily life as a journalist, teacher, citizen, and most of all, I have felt his absence in my awareness of being a literary orphan."

Inasmuch as our stories are the bastard children of everything that we have ever experienced and read, my desire to tell some of my stories in a collaged manner, to merge my own narratives with the oral and written narratives of others, begins with my reading of the two books I eagerly checked out from the Livres Haitiens section of the Brooklyn Public Library that day, books that could have been written only by literary orphans, to offer to other literary orphans.

Maxims about judging a book by its cover aside, when I picked up Jan J. Dominique's *Mémoire d'une amnésique*, I was of course drawn to its paradoxical title. How can an amnesiac remember? Perhaps there is a particular type of memory allowed to amnesiacs, one that only other amnesiacs or near amnesiacs share. I had grown up steeped in Haitian orality, but I had never seen it written down in French before, especially in such an intricate and graceful way. Here was a deeply moving exploration of childhood, of a complex father/daughter relationship, further complicated by a brutal dictator who to his arsenal of physiological weapons adds folktales, turning old myths into living nightmares. Thus the legend of the Tonton Macoutes, bogeymen who come to take disobedient children away in a knapsack, comes to life in the form of denim-clad killers, henchmen and henchwomen who would assassinate their own mothers and fathers if so ordered by the dictator.

A foreign journalist once asked François Duvalier what he represented for Haitians and Duvalier replied that he was their father and the Virgin Mary was their mother. Duvalier also dressed as the guardian of cemetery, the Baron Samedi, and was believed to have stealthily stood in the crowd dressed like this, or in military camouflage, at the public execution of Marcel Numa and Louis Drouin. Thus all Haitians were meant to be like the future young writer of Jan J.'s novel, terrified children who could not be sure even whom to look in the eye or smile at or love. For love could easily turn into something ugly, something that could be expressed only through violence. A slap, like the one given to the daughter who must not speak against the evil she witnesses, to silence her and protect her from greater injuries. Coldness that hides a fear of attachment because who knows when we might have to leave, to go into hiding, into exile? Who knows when we might have to die? Who knows if we are going to be remembered once we are gone?

Grappling with memory is, I believe, one of many complicated Haitian obsessions. We have, it seems, a collective agreement to remember our triumphs and gloss over our failures. Thus, we speak of the Haitian revolution as though it happened just yesterday but we rarely speak of the slavery that prompted it. Our paintings show glorious Eden-like African jungles but never the Middle Passage. In order to shield our shattered collective psyche from a long history of setbacks and disillusionment, our constant roller-coaster ride between saviors and dictators, homespun oppression and foreign tyranny, we cultivate communal and historical amnesia, continually repeating cycles that we never see coming until we are reliving similar horrors.

Never again will foreigners trample Haitian soil, the founders of the republic declared in 1804. Yet in 1915, the "boots," as they are referred to in Jan J.'s novel, invade, launching an American occupation that would last nineteen years. As soon as they landed, U.S. marines shut down the press, took charge of Haiti's banks and customhouses, and instituted a system of compulsory labor for poor Haitians. By the end of the occupation, more than fifteen thousand Haitians had lost their lives.

"The United States is at war with Haiti," W. E. B. Dubois wrote after returning from a fact-finding mission to occupied Haiti. "Congress has never sanctioned the war. Josephus Daniels [President Woodrow Wilson's secretary of the navy] has illegally and unjustly occupied a free foreign land and murdered its inhabitants by the thousands. He has deposed its officials and dispersed its legally elected representatives. He is carrying on a reign of terror, brow-beating, and cruelty, at the hands of southern white naval officers and Marines. For more than a year this red-handed deviltry has proceeded, and today the Island is in open rebellion."

Growing up in the shadow of that rebellion, the narrator's father will never truly know a free and sovereign life, having had not just his country but also his imagination invaded as a small boy when his parents used the presence of U.S. marines to frighten him into drinking his milk.

There are many ways that our mind protects us from present and past horrors. One way is by allowing us to forget. Forgetting is a constant fear in any writer's life. For the immigrant writer, far from home, memory becomes an even deeper abyss. It is as if we had been forced to step under the notorious forgetting trees, the *sabliyes*, that our slave ancestors were told would remove their past from their heads and dull their desire to return home. We know we must pass under the tree, but we hold our breath and cross our fingers and toes and hope that the forgetting will not penetrate too deeply into our brains.

But what happens when we cannot tell our own stories, when our memories have temporarily abandoned us? What is left is longing for something we are not even sure we ever had but are certain we will never experience again.

"I love memories on glossy paper," the struggling novelist narrator of *Mémoire d'une amnésique* declares. Memories when not frozen in time are excruciating, yet Jan J.'s stand-in writer has no choice but to write around these memories because, for one thing, the types of books she loves and would love to write are forbidden and illegal. Their mere presence in her house can result in the arrest and execution of her entire family.

How does one write under those conditions? this novel asks again and again. How can we not write in code, *andaki*, when so many of those who came before us lost their lives because they thought they had nothing to fear? How does Jan J. write after having seen her father gunned down a few feet from where they worked together at his radio station? The book that she finally began writing three years after his death is called *Mémoire errante*, Wandering Memory.

In *Mémoire errante*, Jan J., now as a memoirist, writes, "Since April 3, 2000, I no longer write. Before I was full of ideas. I have always loved working on many texts at once, planning parallel stories. A story set in the present filled with furor and noise while dreaming of a woman from the past without knowing if the two will eventually become linked. There has been no link. There has been no book."

A book that almost never was is *Amour, colère, folie*, the single-volume trilogy I encountered on my next trip to my Livres Haitiens haven at the Brooklyn public library. The author was the stunning and brave—the *guapa*—Marie Vieux-Chauvet. Born in Port-au-Prince during the first year of the U.S. occupation, she would later recreate this period in *Love*, the first novella in her seminal trilogy, which was published for the first time in English in August 2009 as *Love, Anger, Madness*. Claire Clamont, the main character of *Love*, equates her own unfortunate predicament as a thirty-nine-year-old virgin with the predicaments of D. H. Lawrence's Lady Chatterley and Flaubert's Madame Bovary (both Vieux-Chauvet favorites) when she laments in her journal that "there is hunger of the body and that of the soul. And the hunger of the mind and the hunger of the senses. All sufferings are equal."

But is all suffering equal, Marie Vieux-Chauvet wonders, when the people who suffer are not considered equal? How do those who stuff hot potatoes into their child servants' mouths fare against those who murder a journalist or rape a neighbor? How can those who have been brutally enslaved turn around and enslave others? Is suffering truly equal when we live in a society that would never allow the people who are suffering to be considered equal?

"We have been practicing at cutting each other's throats since Independence," Vieux-Chauvet writes of the country that we Haitians like to remind the world was the first black republic in the Western Hemisphere, home to the only slave revolt that succeeded in producing a nation. What we would rather not say, and what Vieux-Chauvet does, is that this same country has continued to fail to reach its full potential, in part because of foreign interference, but also because of internal strife and cruelty.

X, the pseudonymous town featured in *Love*, is terrorized by local henchmen who are given by an unseen dictator the power to decide at any time who lives and who dies. The town is also plagued by other terrors. Not only are the hills and mountains heartbreakingly eroded, but American ships routinely leave X's ports filled with prized wood from trees the loss of which is causing that erosion. Children die of typhoid and malaria. Beggars drink dirty water from ditches and are routinely persecuted by the ruling colonel. Even though this section of the trilogy is mostly set in the 1930s, it is obvious that it is meant also to evoke the later period, 1967, during which this book was written in a six-month-long writing binge—when the elder Duvalier's regime was becoming more and more severe and, in addition to carrying out public and private executions, was persecuting intellectuals and artists.

"Alone again," Marie Vieux-Chauvet writes, referring to Rose Normil of *Anger*, the second novella in the trilogy, "she had invented touchingly naïve myths to console herself: a leaf whirling in the wind, a butterfly whether black or multicolored, the hooting of an owl or the graceful song of a nightingale seemed pregnant with meaning."

This is me, I thought, reading this while attempting my first little stories filled with my self-created folklore—my fake-lore—my hybrid and *métisse* warm-weather daffodils, my crackling fires of dried tree branches and death-announcing black butterflies, my visions of flame-feathered birds.

It is in *Madness*, the final novella of the trilogy, that Vieux-Chauvet perhaps comes closest to reproducing *herself* and her dilemma as a writer living and writing under a brutal authoritarian regime. Depicting four persecuted poets living in a shack, she echoes her own membership in Les Araignées du soir (Spiders of the Night), a small group of poets and novelists who met weekly at her house to discuss one another's work. Like actual spiders, they hoped to weave a protective web around their own and keep out predatory pests. But many were either jailed or exiled by the dictatorship, and Marie Vieux-Chauvet herself had no choice but to flee Haiti in 1968, after this book, on the verge of being published in Paris, was pulled from publication for fear that her family members might be arrested or killed.

According to Rose-Myriam Réjouis, one of the trilogy's two official translators, when Marie Vieux-Chauvet received news that the book had been accepted for publication, she threw a party at which she read excerpts from her manuscript to her friends and family.

"It was then," writes Réjouis, "that family and friends expressed concerns about how the book might, no matter what absurd formula Duvalier used to determine who counted as an enemy of the state, put the life of every member of her family and her husband's family at risk."

At first Marie Vieux-Chauvet resisted, insisting that the publication of the book might bring rebuke and shame to the regime, but then it became obvious that she would have to choose between the book and the people she loved.

"There is a curious split in my behavior," the poet narrator of *Madness* confesses. "I calmly go where there is screaming, where I am certain the devils are committing murder. I avoid danger while accusing myself of cowardice, loathing my own reactions. In the trunk there are a few poems, unpublished, as are all of my poems about devils and hell. Enough of them there to get me pumped full of lead without anyone hesitating."

Exile became Marie Vieux-Chauvet's only choice.

Later, while living in Queens, New York, Marie Vieux-Chauvet wrote *Les Rapaces* (The Vultures), a novel that portrays a writer wrestling with his work and his brutal surroundings after the death of Papa Doc Duvalier. Through the valiant effort of a devoted reader, the work of that book's fictional writer manages to live on, something that Marie Vieux-Chauvet must have dreamed of for herself while writing about Haiti, in French, in the United States, not certain if either she or her books would ever find their way back to Haiti or would ever find an interested audience in the United States.

On June 19, 1973, at fifty-seven years old, Marie Vieux-Chauvet died of brain cancer after five years in exile. The Duvalier dictatorship had been passed down from father to son, whom the U.S. government saw as more acceptable. Foreign investment flowed into Haiti, nurturing an atrocious sweatshop culture that added another layer of despair to the lives of a population that could not refuse to work, no matter how meager the pay. Other poor Haitians were sold by the Haitian government in secret deals to work in the sugarcane fields of the Dominican Republic and were shipped off like slaves to the other side of the island.

As a child growing up in Haiti at the time, I heard, along with the darkest of tales of the brutal Tonton Macoutes or Vieux-Chauvet's men in black, stories of children being kidnapped so their organs could be harvested and used to save rich sick children in America, an idea that frightened me so much that I sometimes could not sleep. What would Marie Vieux-Chauvet have made of such a tale? I wonder. Or of the period that followed the end of the Duvalier dictatorship, when the son flew off into his own exile and the people, like the beggars of her trilogy and the masses of *Les Rapaces*, took to the streets in celebration and revenge? What would she have made of the first democratically elected president of Haiti, or the death of Jean Dominique? Of September 11th? Of Haiti's catastrophic earthquake on January 12, 2010? And what would it have been like to have sat down with her over a cup of coffee in a dark corner of a Haitian restaurant in Port-au-Prince or Miami, as I have had the pleasure of doing with Jan J. Dominique? In Marie Vieux-Chauvet's absence, I feel orphaned. But it was only after I read Jan J.'s *Mémoire errante* that I felt once again what it was like to lose a literary parent and a biological one at the same time.

Because she bore her father's name but for a single vowel, there was always the possibility that someone would mistake the novelist daughter for the agronomist/journalist. So the novelist daughter at first used her nickname, J. J., on the cover of her books.

"One day they'll introduce me as the father of Jan, the novelist," her father said. He loved her novels. He said that one of them reminded him of Proust, his favorite writer. "If I weren't your father," he said, "I'd write a review, but people would think me biased."

Then there was the assassination and her being unable to write because everyone was saying to her, "You should write about your father," which she eventually did.

For her part, during the final months of her life, Marie Vieux-Chauvet was researching and mapping out an epic novel called *Les Enfants d'Ogoun* (The Children of Ogoun), Ogoun being the Haitian god of war. Unfortunately, Marie Vieux-Chauvet died before completing more than a few pages of this much hoped-for book.

"I would like to be sure," she writes in *Love*, "that Beethoven died appeased that he had written his concertos. Without this certainty, what would be the point of the painful anxiety of a Cézanne searching for a color that escapes him? Or of the anguish of a Dostoyevsky grasping at God in the thoughts swarming within the hellish complexity of the soul!"

I too would like to be sure that Marie Vieux-Chauvet died appeased that she, like her living sister novelist/memoirist Jan J. Dominique, had written, passionately, fearlessly, dangerously, the books that she did. The more I write myself, the more certain I am that she did.

I Speak Out

Alèrte Bélance: I only have a stub where my arm used to be, and the fingers of my left hand have been severed; I can't close it. That hand can't do anything for me. That's why I say to you: consider that I always lift my face up, I speak out. . . . Look at my martyrdom from when the wicked ones kidnapped me and took me to the killing fields. . . . Hear my story, what I have experienced.

We were speeding through the Lincoln Tunnel toward New Jersey to visit a Haitian woman named Alèrte Bélance. Alèrte was the latest casualty of the 1991 military coup d'état in Haiti. We—the director, the producers of the documentary, and I— had heard about Alèrte through a refugee women's organization in Brooklyn. We were told that she had been arrested by men belonging to a paramilitary group working for the junta that had led the coup and had become the de facto leadership of the country. Five of us immediately jumped into a small car and, with a trunk full of video equipment, headed for the public housing project in Newark where Alèrte, her husband, and their three children were living. Our documentary was about

Haitian torture survivors and we hoped that she would tell us her story.

As we entered the sparsely furnished apartment on the top floor of the six-story building, we were greeted by two young girls dressed in ruffled pink dresses and matching bows in their hair. Alèrte's son was sitting on a large orange sofa in the middle of the living room. He was a small boy and it was hard to tell whether he was older or younger than the girls, who both appeared to be around ten. The boy never smiled, which made me think that he was indeed older and understood a lot better than his sisters did what had happened.

Alèrte's husband, a youthful-looking, goateed man, carried in a few chairs from the kitchen for us. Then Alèrte emerged from the bedroom. She was a small woman, her dark face sunken on one side where a machete had nearly chopped off her cheekbone. She was in her late twenties, but looked twice as old, the machete scars and suture marks like tiny railroad tracks leading toward her chin. She was wearing a green blouse, a flowered skirt, and a dark knit cap on her head, and as she limped toward the couch she greeted each of us with a nod.

Somewhere downstairs a baby was crying.

"These apartments are sometimes used for battered women," she said in halting Creole.

Still, her voice was a lot clearer than we had expected, since during the attack her tongue had been cut in two.

While lingering on her voice, it was also hard not to stare at her right forearm, the pointy black stub filled with keloid scars. Leading to the tip were more machete scars, as though the person—the people—who had chopped off her arm had tried extremely hard to do it. You could not look at that arm and not wonder where the rest of it was.

My brother Kelly also has a missing forearm. Unlike Alèrte, he was born that way. I am not exactly sure what happened with Kelly, but when my youngest daughter, Leila, was born with a few small indentations in her left earlobe, her pediatrician told me that sometimes in the womb, elongated tissue called amniotic bands wrap themselves so tightly around fetal tissue that they can amputate a fetus's arm or leg. My Vodou- and Santeria-practicing friends, however, tell me that when a person is born missing any piece of flesh—be it a limb or otherwise—it means that the person has lost a twin in the womb and that lost twin has put a visible mark on the living twin.

At last, I'd thought, I had two possible answers to the mystery that was my beautiful brother. Kelly's missing forearm had dissolved inside my mother, becoming a part of the tissue, and spirit, that had helped create him. Alèrte's missing forearm had dissolved in a mass grave, becoming a part of the country that had helped create her.

Alèrte Bélance: They sliced me into pieces with machete strokes. They cut out my tongue and my mouth: my gums, plates, teeth, and jaw on my right side. They cut my face open, my temple and cheek totally open. They cut my eye open. They cut my ear open. They cut my body, my whole shoulder and neck and back slashed with machete blows. They cut off my right arm. They slashed my left arm totally and cut off the ends of all the fingers of my left hand. Also, they slashed my whole head up with machete blows.

Once the lights and cameras were set up, the director, my friend Patricia Benoit, tried to begin gently.

"*Ki jan w ye?*" How are you? Patricia, who was born in Haiti and moved to the United States with her parents when she was six, has a soft, hesitant, but cajoling voice in Creole. Fluent in English, Creole, and French, she is not only trilingual but also tritonal, having a distinctive timbre and pitch for each language she speaks. Patricia has often filmed in Haiti and has seen other victims of other horrors, so when she said to Alèrte, "*Ki jan w ye?*" it did not sound like small talk, especially in this nearly empty room so far from all of our homes.

Alèrte settled on the couch and with her semifunctioning hand began tugging at the dark knit cap on her head. She removed the cap and underneath were more scars and a military-style buzz cut. She quickly put the cap back on.

"We'll do this any way you want," Patricia said softly, "but you look nice with your cap off."

With her cap off, even with the machete scars so visible, Alèrte's injured cheekbones emerged. Her eyes had a glint of onyx and she had a coy smile that came from only one side of her mouth.

"I look like a boy," she said, nervously rolling the cap in her hand.

She asked her husband to get two faux pearl earrings from a box in the bedroom. When he came back, he leaned down and, because she could not, put the earrings on her ears. Then he sat down next to her, as though to shield her from the camera.

What did you do for a living in Haiti?" Patricia asked Alèrte.

"I sold food in the market," she said.

Her husband, she said, was a welder. He was also involved in some neighborhood committees that organized rallies for Jean-Bertrand Aristide when he was a presidential candidate.

Patricia guided her slowly toward the moment when the paramilitary men, called attachés, came to her house in Port-au-Prince.

They wanted to wipe out everyone who'd voted for Aristide, she said. Her husband, because of his election organizing, was targeted. They came knocking on her door. When her husband saw who they were, he escaped through a window in the back of their house. He thought that if they didn't find him they would simply go away. He never thought they'd take her in his place.

They put her in the back of a pickup truck and drove her to a deserted stretch of land outside of town, Haiti's so-called valley of death, a vast mass grave called Titanyen. There two men hacked her with machetes. When she realized that they were trying to kill her, she stopped fighting, lay down, and played dead. She lost the arm, she said, trying to shield her face and the rest of her body.

When the paramilitary men saw that she had stopped moving, one of them said, "Look, it seems like she's dead."

"They had more people to kill," she said, "so they left me there."

She waited until they were gone. Then she dragged herself back to the side of the road and waited until morning.

As she spoke, slowly but firmly, as if reliving every second of these horrors, I wrote a summary translation on a legal pad for one of our non-Creole-speaking producers. I felt tears run down my face. This was perhaps unprofessional, even disrespectful. The telling of that story was such a courageous act, I thought, that only one person in that room had the right to cry.

Alèrte Bélance: I woke up again the next morning and found myself stuck on top of a briar path where the *zenglendo* threw me. My whole body was full of prickers. I didn't feel them, though, because my whole body was dead. I'm not positive where I was because I couldn't see—my eyes were stuck together with blood—but I think I was up in the air, perched on the side of a hill, just over a hole. I felt myself shaking, my whole body was trembling. I unstuck my eyes and then I saw that I wasn't too far from the road. But I couldn't see up or down, I couldn't move to the left or right. Anywhere I turned, I would fall into the hole.

Patricia then moved on to her incredible survival.

"How did you get found?" she asked.

In the morning, on the precipice by the side of the road, she saw many cars speeding by. She stopped to raise her bloody arms to catch their attention. Some drivers, stopped and gawked and then got back into their cars and kept going. By then she was covered with the *pikan*, the thorns that are common in the area. One potential good Samaritan even said, "She's not dead," but kept going. Finally an army pickup truck came by and—proving that not all soldiers are the same—one of the two soldiers in the truck said, "We can't leave that woman here." They picked her up and put her in the back of the truck.

Tearful, Alèrte stopped talking and her husband picked up the narrative from there. During the entire interview, he referred to her in Creole as *dam la*, the lady, a rather formal but not impersonal designation.

After escaping to his aunt's house in another part of town, Alèrte's husband returned home the next morning. The children told him that their mother had been taken away by the men who'd come the night before. That same morning, a soldier came to the house and asked who he was. He hesitantly told the soldier his name. The soldier said, "You should come quick to the hospital. Your wife is sick. She may even die before you get there."

When he got to the hospital, he did not recognize her. "That's not my wife," he told the doctors.

Alèrte had the presence of mind to nod her head to indicate to him that she was indeed Alèrte.

"She had long hair before," he said, pointing to her buzz haircut. "But when I saw her, she was like the chopped meat they sell at the market."

Later a human rights group would publish a brochure filled with pictures of Alèrte taken in the hospital after her attack. I had never seen anything like it: picture after picture of hollowed pockets of severed and swollen tissue all over her face, arms, and legs.

The doctors had to hide her when several attachés came looking for her in the hospital. There were many instances of attachés coming back to kill torture survivors in hospitals. A young man who had been left for dead in Titanyen was later taken to the hospital, and then was murdered in the hospital by paramilitary men as his grandfather watched helplessly. That precedent forced the doctors to hide her.

She was lucky to have had the doctors she had, she chimed in. Doctors like that are hard to come by for poor women in overcrowded hospitals in Haiti. The doctors hid her and, when the killers came by, they would say that she had died.

Slowly, she said, reaching up to touch the scars on the side of her face, she began to heal. But she did not want to give the impression that it was quick and easy, as in a movie. She remembered the infections over her entire body, when most of her wounds were filled with puss. She had to be on oxygen a lot of the time because her nasal cavities were too inflamed to take in enough air.

As she talked, her daughters played nearby. They had heard all this before, it seemed, and they could ignore it now, or they were simply protecting themselves by giggling together on the floor and disturbing the shoot. Their childish giggles reminded Alèrte to say that after all this, after she went from being a plump, voluptuous, long-haired woman to a skinny, buzz-cut amputee, her daughters also did not recognize her. Because of her new appearance, they did not know who she was. The younger of the two would pull a picture from the side of the bed, a framed picture of Alèrte looking fleshy and healthy and smiling. The child would carry the picture to her and say, "You are not my mother. This is my mother."

It took the children a while to get used to her new body and the new, deeper voice she had as a result of her tongue having been cut in half and sewn back together again. The tongue had been hanging by a thread of flesh, but the doctors sewed it back on and, miraculously, it healed.

"It healed," she said, "so I can tell my story, so people can know what happened to me."

Her strength and resolve seemed to grow with each word, even as she said she got depressed sometimes because she couldn't do much for herself or her family. She ached all the time from the wounds we could see and others we could not see. At night she ached even more because of the *seren*, the twilight air, which affected her bones. Her husband had to bathe her and comb the children's hair. Something a man ought not to have to do, she added.

Her son was sitting quietly in a corner observing the shoot while her daughters played and ate candy in their Sunday dresses. Watching the girls, it occurred to me that when they are grown, they may look exactly the way their mother used to look.

"I think we are done," Patricia said at the end of the interview.

Alèrte's body slid down on the couch. She seemed relieved. Her eyes traveled around the room, and then she asked Patricia, "*Kote w soti?*" Where are you from?

Patricia told of her origins in shorthand. Born in Haiti. Mother French. Father Haitian. Raised in Queens.

"Do you like New Jersey?" Patricia asked.

She did not go out much, Alèrte said. People stared. She had just been invited to appear on the *Phil Donahue Show*, though, and had agreed to go and, with a translator, tell her story.

"If it helps Haiti," she said.

Suddenly, her son edged closer. Patricia asked him if he wanted to say something.

The boy said yes.

On camera?

The boy nodded.

Patricia asked Alèrte and her husband if it was all right to let the boy speak on camera.

They both nodded.

We started filming again, and the shy little boy told of seeing his mother in the hospital for the first time.

"She looked like chopped meat," he said, echoing his father's words.

Tears ran down the little boy's face as he spoke. His body was tense but it seemed as if he was finally releasing a knot in his stomach. He could not stop crying.

We all began to cry along with him, even those who did not speak Creole and could not understand a word he said.

As we drove back though the Lincoln Tunnel, leaving Alèrte and her family behind, we all wondered if there was more we could have said. Was there something else we could have done? I kept asking myself what Alèrte's life with her husband was now like, what their relationship was like beyond his being helpful to her. A question I could not ask was whether or not they were still attracted to each other, still in love.

A few months later I got my answer.

She became pregnant.

Alèrte Bélance: I remember lying in the hospital bed and
   trying to imagine how I was going to live in the situation

I'm in now. I don't have two arms. My left arms sticks to my body but serves no purpose for me. . . . Killing Alèrte Bélance was supposed to mean that Alèrte Bélance couldn't speak for a better life. Contrary to their stopping me, I'm progressing because I'm still bearing children. They tried to take my life away, but not only couldn't they do that, I'm producing more life.

The following week was the taping of the *Phil Donahue Show*. The producers of the *Donahue Show* asked our producers to find Haitian audience members, and Patricia and I, along with Jean Dominique and a few other friends, were in the audience.

The point of the show was to encourage the Clinton administration to do something about the junta that was killing or maiming people like Alèrte. The lure was the celebrity supporters of Haiti, including Harry Belafonte, Susan Sarandon, and Danny Glover, as well as the TransAfrica Forum founder Randall Robinson, who went on a hunger strike to press the Clinton administration to act. Alèrte did not get to speak very much on the show because she had to use a translator, which slowed down the process of telling her story. Instead, Phil Donahue held her arm up in the air; her story was told more visually than in her own voice.

After the show aired, however, Alèrte became the face of the junta's atrocities in Haiti. I ran into her again at several events and rallies where she loudly demanded the return of the democratically elected government. At one rally, she even shared the stage with President Jean-Bertrand Aristide, who had requested to meet her.

Later, she faced off with some paramilitary leaders on Haitian radio in New York and, with the Center for Constitutional Rights, filed a thirty-two-million-dollar lawsuit against FRAPH, the paramilitary organization to which the attachés who'd attacked her belonged. More than a decade later, the case against FRAPH was decided in her favor, but it is unlikely that she will ever recover a dime.

As her visibility grew, she was featured in several U.S. newspapers and magazines and got a small speaking part in the Jonathan Demme–directed film version of Toni Morrison's *Beloved*. In the film, Alèrte plays Nan, a woman "who used different words." Jonathan Demme had Alèrte say Nan's lines ("She threw them all away but you") in Haitian Creole, to the lead character, Sethe, played by Oprah Winfrey.

When one first saw Alèrte Bélance, what was most visible about her were her "marks," her scars. But eventually it was also easy to recognize her spirited defiance.

"Do you realize how strong you are?" Patricia had asked her.

"Yes, I realize that I am strong," she replied. "I am very strong. Some people get a small cut and it gets infected and they die. Look what was done to me and still I survived. Yes, I am very strong."

In *Courage and Pain*, the undistributed documentary we ended up making, Alèrte and her family are surrounded by nearly a dozen other survivors who, like Alèrte, were nearly executed. They all tell different versions of the same story, of being beaten, macheted, shot, and tortured, and of nearly dying in a country they loved but where they could no longer live.

A few months later, a resolute Alèrte retold her story to Beverly Bell, an American researcher, democracy and women's advocate, who would later compile the excerpts I have quoted throughout this chapter in an oral history titled *Walking on Fire*.

"Three months after I came back from the dead at Titanyen, I was on my two feet," Alèrte told Beverly Bell. "I traveled around the United States trying to beat up on the misery of Haiti and the Haitian people. I spoke about women whom the cruel death and terror gangs were raping, little children they were raping, babies in the cradle. I went on television and the radio; I talked to U.S. congressmen, journalists, human rights activists. I spoke at demonstrations, press conferences, churches, congressional hearings ... to say, "Here. Here is what I suffered."

She not only suffered, however, but against all odds she also survived and thrived. And her testimony was a great gift to many others who were still trying to stay alive, and to the more than eight thousand others who died under the junta's rule.

Alèrte Bélance: They killed mother after mother of children.
They killed doctor after doctor, student after student.
Mothers of children lost their children. . . . The devil has raped the confidence of the people. . . . People of conscience, hear me who is trying to wake you up. Hear my story, what I have experienced . . .

CHAPTER 6

The Other Side of the Water

In the summer of 1997, I flew to Port-au-Prince from New York a few days after my cousin Marius had flown in the cargo section of a similar American Airlines jet from Miami. Once I'd slept past the first half hour after takeoff, I'd strapped on the free headphones and chosen from the in-flight radio selection a pop station playing a song by the rock group Midnight Oil.

> How can we dance when our earth is turning?
> How can we sleep while . . .

Across the aisle from me, a man in a wrinkled brown suit shuffled a few papers in and out of a large manila envelope onto the tray table in front of him. He wiped his brow with a monogrammed blue handkerchief and then rang the flight attendant call button. When a plump blond woman hurried over, he asked her for a glass of water. When she brought it to him, he asked her when we were going to land.

I recognized the man, who had been escorted by immigration officers past the security checkpoint, right through the gate and to his seat on the airplane. He seemed to be in his late forties, was russet brown and thin with a gaunt face, his jaws speckled with the remnants of a beard that looked as though a shave had been attempted on it but had failed. He was a deportee.

While looking over at him, I thought of my cousin Marius, who in his own way had also been deported. I had foreseen the two of us, Marius and me, traveling on the same day and my New York flight arriving a few hours before his Miami one so that I could be there to greet him at the airport in Port-au-Prince, but the obstacles to Marius's flight had been abruptly lifted and some obstacles to mine had abruptly surfaced and Marius had gone ahead on his own, before me, to be buried.

Originally, Marius's departure had been delayed because the undertaker could not locate his papers. Before his mother called us in New York—from Haiti—to announce his death to my father and to ask for our help in getting the body sent to her from Miami, I hadn't seen or spoken to Marius in years. Only two years younger than he was, I had barely interacted with him when I was a girl because his parents had divorced when I was quite young and he lived mostly with his father, who'd rarely mingled with our family. My father could barely remember Marius at all, as he was still a boy when Papa left Haiti for the United States. A decade after I'd moved to the United States, I heard that Marius had taken a boat to Miami. A few days before my flight from New York to Port-au-Prince, his mother had called to tell us that he was dead.

Once he'd offered his condolences to Tante Zi over the phone, my father asked me to pick up the extension and tell her that I would take care of things, would get Marius's body sent to her in Haiti.

After offering my own condolences to a tearful and hiccupping Tante Zi, I asked her where Marius was living before he died.

She paused as if to breathe past a large lump in her throat, and then whispered, "Miami," sounding puzzled, as if wondering why I was making her repeat something she'd already repeated many times.

"Do you have the address of the place where he was living in Miami?" I asked.

"No," she said. But she did have the telephone number of Marius's roommate of two years. His name was Delens.

I would call Delens, I told her, and get back to her.

I dialed Delens's number soon after I hung up with Tante Zi and asked in Creole if I could speak with him. The young man who answered replied, "Would you mind speaking English? I grew up here. It's hard for me to speak Creole."

It turned out that he was Delens. I told him, in English, that I was Marius's cousin and was trying to help locate his body to send it back to Port-au-Prince. Could he help me?

He gave me the number of the Freeman Funeral Home, where Marius's body had already been placed while awaiting expatriation. He didn't have the amount of money the funeral home charged and Tante Zi didn't trust him enough to send it to him, accusing him of being responsible—in some way that he could neither comprehend nor explain—for Marius's death.

At the end of the conversation, I cautiously asked Delens in my most polite voice, "Can you please tell me what Marius died of?"

"*Move maladi ya,*" he responded in perfectly enunciated, nonaccented Creole. The bad disease, a euphemism for acquired immune deficiency syndrome, or AIDS.

"When did it happen?" I asked. "When did he get it?"

"I don't know." He switched back to hip-hop-toned English. "Maybe he had it even before he left Haiti. I don't know. But he's been living wild here, man, made some stupid-ass mistakes."

"Did he leave anything behind?" I thought Tante Zi might want to know. Maybe he had some assets that could help mitigate the transportation and funeral costs. But I wasn't thinking only about money. Perhaps there were more personal effects, legal papers, letters, photographs, journals, keepsakes that later on might comfort his mother.

"He had nothing," Delens replied harshly. "He was living it up and wasted everything. All he had when he died was sixty dollars."

Rightly or wrongly, I couldn't accept that a thirty-year-old man had left nothing else behind. When I hung up and summarized the other end of the conversation for my father, he told me that Tante Zi believed that Marius had been poisoned by his roommate, but almost everyone in the family had different theories. There were those who thought he had committed suicide and others who were certain he'd died of a drug overdose. I didn't know what or whom to believe, but it really didn't matter. A grieving mother was waiting to be reunited with her son. And since she couldn't come to him, we had to find some way to bring him to her.

The funeral, if held in Miami, would cost three thousand dollars, Mr. Freeman told me when I called. But for Marius's body to be shipped back to Haiti, the price would go up to five thousand. He'd already had Marius for a day or two now and would be happy to ship him to the funeral home of our choice anywhere in the Haitian capital, but he needed "papers."

"What kind of papers?" I asked.

Because Marius had come to Miami by boat and had never received asylum or legalized his status some other way, he was undocumented.

"I have to get him exit papers from the Haitian consulate," explained Mr. Freeman. "The U.S. authorities will want to see these papers at the airport before he leaves and the Haitian authorities will want to see them when he arrives."

"He's a dead man whose cadaver needs to be shipped to the country where he was born. Why is it so complicated?" I asked.

"In part," he answered calmly, "because he's an alien."

Were we still aliens in death, I asked, our corpses unwanted visitors still?

Fortunately, Delens managed to find Marius's Haitian passport, so Marius would certainly be granted exit papers by the Haitian consulate, Mister Freeman assured me. It was simply a matter of time.

"But that's not the only thing," he continued in the same unruffled ministerial voice. "It's also complicated because of the disease he died of. There are some special procedures involved with these types of corpses."

Even though it was probably written in large bold letters on Marius's death certificate, no one wanted to name the disease that had killed him. It was as if in some bizarre way they were all respecting his dying wish. Silence at all costs.

The next day, I called Tante Zi and explained all that I'd learned about Marius's return to Haiti. Tante Zi was aware of the funeral home cost, she said; she just wanted to confirm that

Delens was telling the truth. She was ready to make a money transfer. She even had Mister Freeman's information.

"Marius should be home soon," my father told her.

Before she hung up, Tante Zi began sobbing again and then added, "Look how they took my boy from me and took everything he owned on top of it."

Marius had been sending her a few hundred dollars each month, Tante Zi said. There was no way he could have been broke. And he didn't die of the "bad disease" either. He'd called her once a week, every Sunday, and promised her he'd come back to see her as soon as his papers were in order. During those talks, he was always full of laughter and hope. He never sounded like a sick person.

My father abruptly interrupted Tante Zi's tearful recollection and told her to calm down, to make sure she had her head on straight so she could face what lay ahead.

"You haven't seen your son in years," he reminded her. "He's coming back to you in a coffin. *Met fanm sou ou.* Be the strong woman you have to be."

Tante Zi, who often openly said that she loved my father more than all her other siblings—just as she said of all her other siblings that she loved them more than the others—agreed.

"You're right, brother," she said, still sniffling in my ear on the other extension. "I'll have to pull myself together to face this."

"I am sorry I can't come there to be with you," my father, who was recovering from very early symptoms of the pulmonary fibrosis that would eventually kill him, said to Tante Zi.

"I understand, brother," she said.

Three days later, Marius's exit papers came in. After eight days in Mister Freeman's morgue, Marius was going home. In the meantime, my father had a sudden crisis with his health and I missed Marius's departure day. Marius's body was shipped to Port-au-Prince. I missed his arrival in and his wake and burial, too.

When I got to Haiti, I didn't immediately visit the family mausoleum where Marius was buried. I didn't have to. Tante Zi had had the entire funeral photographed and a small souvenir album made. The most eye-catching pictures were of Marius lying in his silver coffin in a dark suit and tie, his hands carefully folded on top of his belly. His dark bloated pancake face was sculpted around a half grin that makes it hard to imagine what he might have looked like under different circumstances.

I saw Tante Zi several times that summer in Haiti, once at the baptism of her newest granddaughter, the child of her only daughter, Marie. She also came to visit me at the seaside campus where I was working, helping to teach a college course to American students.

One afternoon when she came to visit, we sat on the warm sand under an almond tree as two of my Haitian cousins played soccer and water volleyball with some of the students in the course. We watched the calm turquoise sea and bare brown mountains in the distance, the clouds shifting ever so carefully above them, rationing sunshine and shade. I knew that Marius would come up at some point that afternoon, and he did.

"I know this is what you do now," Tante Zi said. "This thing with the writing. I know it's your work, but please don't write what you think you know about Marius."

The truth is that I knew very little about Marius. Even though we were cousins, the same blood, our adult lives—my adult life, his adult death—might never have intersected at all had I not been asked to help return his body home. In the end, there had been very little drama even in this returning of his body. It was all so sanitized, so over-the-phone, nothing *Antigone* about it.

This type of thing happened all the time, Mr. Freeman and Delens had each explained to me in his own way: faraway family members realize that they are discovering—or recovering—in death fragments of a life that had swirled in hidden stories. In Haiti the same expression, *lòt bò dlo*, the other side of the water, can be used to denote the eternal afterlife as well as an émigré's eventual destination. It is sometimes impossible even for those of us who are on the same side of *lòt bò dlo* to find one another.

"We have still not had a death," Marquez's Colonel says. "A person does not belong to a place until someone is dead under the ground." Does that person still belong if someone died there, but is not buried under that ground?

"You should be buried where you die," Tante Zi's older sister, Tante Ilyana, had said. But what if you are all alone where you die? What if all your kin is *lòt bò dlo*?

"People talk," Tante Zi went on. "They say that everything they say to you ends up written down somewhere."

Because she was my elder, my beloved aunt, I bowed my head in shame, wishing I could apologize for that, but noble silences aside, this immigrant artist, like many other artists, is a leech and I needed to latch on. I wanted to quote the French poet and critic Stéphane Mallarmé and tell her that everything in the world exists to end up in a book. I wanted to ask her forgiveness for the essay that in my mind I was already writing. The most I could do, however, was to promise her not to use her real name or Marius's.

She was silent again, momentarily comforted by that tiny compromise. I changed the subject, asking if she wanted to go swimming. Just to relax her body a little, I said, before the return trip from the resort town where I was teaching, back to Port-au-Prince. I thought she would say no. She had turned me down before. Still I hoped that she might surprise me and say yes.

"I can't," she began, and then corrected herself. "I don't want to."

A large cloud lingered above, casting a hint of gray over us. But it was still sunny over the water, the waves glittering as though taunting the fogginess above.

"Some people come back from the other side of the water, don't they?" She said, her eyes still fixed on the water. "You're proof of that, *non*?"

She raised her hands high in the air, aiming them at the twinkling sea as if to both scold and embrace it.

"They do," I said.

"Why didn't Marius come back?" She seemed to be asking both me and the sea.

"I don't know," I said.

"It's stupid to even ask," she said, scratching the short gray hair under the white kerchief that covered her head. "How could any of us know the answer to something like that? Only the sea and God know. Right?"

"Right," I echoed, still treading carefully after her rebuke.

"I suppose I should be glad we didn't lose him at sea," she said.

With her eyes still on the water, she got up and peeled off her milky white clothes. Wearing only her red bra and dark panties, she walked toward the ocean for an afternoon swim.

CHAPTER 7

Bicentennial

Two hundred years had passed since the Western Hemisphere's second republic was created. Back then, there were no congratulatory salutes from the first, the United States of America. The new republic, Haiti, had gained its independence through a bloody twelve-year slave uprising, the only time in the history of the world that bond servants successfully overthrew their masters and formed their own state.

The two young nations had several things in common. Both had been heavily taxed colonies, and both had visionary leaders whose words had the power to inspire men to fight. Compare, for example, Thomas Jefferson's vision of the tree of liberty as one that must be "refreshed from time to time with the blood of patriots and tyrants" with that of the Haitian general Toussaint L'Ouverture who, as he was captured by the French and was being taken to his death, declared, "In overthrowing me they have only felled the tree of Negro liberty.... It will shoot up again, for it is deeply rooted and its roots are many."

The fact that the United States of America was not more supportive of its smaller, slightly younger neighbor had a great deal to do with L'Ouverture's roots, which were African and which were now planted in America's backyard. Thomas Jefferson, who had drafted the declaration that defined his own nation's insurgency and who had witnessed and praised the French Revolution, knew exactly what revolutions meant. Their essence was not in their instantaneous bursts of glory but in their ripple effect across borders and time, their ability to put the impossible within reach and make the downtrodden seem mighty. And he feared that Haiti's revolt would inspire similar actions in the United States. "If something is not done, and soon done, we shall be the murderers of our own children," Jefferson wrote about the potential impact of the Haitian uprising.

Haiti's very existence highlighted the deepest contradictions of the American revolutionary experiment. The U.S. Declaration of Independence stated that all men were created equal, but Haitian slaves and free men and women of color battled what was then one of the world's most powerful armies to prove it. Yet how could the man who wrote about freedom in such transcendent terms have failed to hear echoes of his own country's revolutionary struggle, and victory, in the Haitians' urgent desire for self-rule? Possibly because as a slaveowner and the leader of slaveholders he couldn't manage to reconcile dealing with one group of Africans as leaders and another as chattel. So Haiti's independence remained unrecognized by Thomas Jefferson, who urged Congress to suspend commerce with the nascent nation, declaring its leaders "cannibals of the terrible republic."

Timothy Pickering, a senator from Massachusetts who had served as John Adams's secretary of state, wrote to Jefferson to protest his refusal to aid the new Haitian republic. "Are these men not merely to be abandoned to their own efforts but to be deprived of those necessary supplies which for a series of years, they have been accustomed to receive from the United States, and without which they cannot subsist?" Pickering asked.

Yet the United States had benefited greatly from the colonial strife next door. Broke after its Haitian defeat, France sold a large region, 828,000 square miles, from the western banks of the Mississippi River to the Rocky Mountains, to the United States for fifteen million dollars. The Louisiana Purchase would prove to be one of the most profitable real estate transactions ever made, nearly doubling the size of the United States at a cost of about four cents an acre. Alexander Hamilton said Napoleon would not have sold his claims except for the "courage and obstinate resistance [of the] black inhabitants" of Haiti.

It would take six decades for the United States to acknowledge Haiti's independence. During that time, Haiti continued to be considered as a possible penal colony for the United States or as a place (à la Liberia) where freed blacks could be repatriated. By the time Abraham Lincoln recognized Haiti's independence in 1862, America was already at war with itself over the issue of slavery. Burdened by its postindependence isolation and the hundred million francs in payment it was forced to give France for official recognition—an amount estimated to be worth more than twenty-two billion U.S. dollars today, which some Haitians, including the former president Jean-Bertrand Aristide, have insisted should be repaid—Haiti began its perilous slide toward turmoil and dependency, resulting in a nineteen-year U.S. occupation and three subsequent interventions in the past hundred years.

CHAPTER 7

In *Notes on the State of Virginia*, Thomas Jefferson predicts what might happen to the U.S. political system in a worst-case scenario. But his words turned out to be a more accurate prophecy for America's plundered neighbor. "The spirit of the times ... will alter," Jefferson wrote. "Our rulers will become corrupt. ... The shackles ... which shall not be knocked off at the conclusion of war will remain on long, will be made heavier and heavier."

Perhaps, had it been given a fair chance at its beginning, Haiti might have flourished and prospered. If that had been the case, Haiti might have celebrated the bicentennial of its independence with fewer shackles. Instead, in January 2004, Haiti observed the two-hundredth anniversary of its independence from France in the midst of a national revolt. In the Haitian capital and other cities throughout the country, pro- and antigovernment demonstrators clashed. Members of a disbanded army declared war on a young and inexperienced police force. Mobs of angry young men, some called *chimè* (chimeras) by their countrymen and others ironically echoing Thomas Jefferson and calling themselves *lame kanibal*, the cannibal army, battled one another to determine whether the then Haitian president Jean-Bertrand Aristide—worshipped by chimeras and reviled by the cannibal army—would remain in office or be overthrown.

A few weeks later, Aristide departed in the early hours of a Sunday morning. By his account, he was kidnapped from his residence in Port-au-Prince and put on an unmarked U.S. jet, which took him to the Central African Republic, where he was practically held prisoner for several weeks. By other accounts, he went willingly, even signing a letter of resignation in Haitian Creole. What remains uncontested is that as he began his life in exile, Aristide recited for the international press the same words that Toussaint L'Ouverture uttered on his way to mortal exile in France: "In overthrowing me they have only felled the tree of Negro liberty.... It will shoot up again, for it is deeply rooted and its roots are many"

Haitians in and outside of Haiti were not surprised that, in Haiti's bicentennial year, Aristide chose to link his exit with such a powerful echo from the past. After all, there has never been a more evocative moment in Haiti's history—even though neglected by the world—than the triumphant outcome of the revolution that L'Ouverture and others had lived and died for exactly two hundred years earlier. Though Haiti's transition from slavery to free state was far from seamless, many Haitians, myself included, would rather forget the divisions that followed independence, the color and class biases that split the country into sections ruled by self-declared oligarchs and monarchs who governed exactly as they had been governed, with little regard for parity or autonomy.

In *The Kingdom of This World*, the Cuban novelist Alejo Carpentier allows us to consider the possibility, with which his own Cuba would later grapple, that a revolution that some consider visionary might appear to others to have failed. Through the eyes of Ti Noël, no king or ruler but rather an ordinary man, we get an intimate view of the key players in an epic story that merges myth and lore, magical realism with historical facts. Here we encounter some of the most memorable architects of the Haitian revolution, along with some fictional comrades they pick up along the way. We meet the one-armed Makandal, who is said to have turned into a million fireflies, or in other accounts a mere insect, in order to escape his fiery execution by French colonists. We also meet a Jamaican expatriate, Bouckman—most commonly spelled Boukman—who presided over the stirring Vodou ceremony that helped transform young Toussaint L'Ouverture from a mild-mannered herbalist to a heroic warrior. And of course we come to know King Christophe, a former restaurateur, who later shoots himself with a silver bullet, but not before forcing his countrymen to experience "the rebirth of shackles, this proliferation of suffering, which the more resigned began to accept as proof of the uselessness of all revolt."

Though Ti Noël does not remain among the resigned for too long, he is certainly tested through his disheartening encounters with those who have shaped his country's destiny. Like Haiti itself, he cannot be fully defined. At best one might see Ti Noël as a stand-in for the novelist Carpentier. Born of a Russian mother and a French father, Carpentier shows with his skillful handling of this narrative how revolutions assign us all sides, shaming the conquerors and fortifying the oppressed, and in some cases achieving the opposite. For even if history is most often recounted by victors, it's not always easy to tell who the rightful narrators should be, unless we keep redefining with each page what it means to conquer and be conquered.

Of Carpentier's Cuba, Thomas Jefferson wrote, "I candidly confess that I have ever looked on Cuba as the most interesting addition which could ever be made to our system of States. The control which, with Florida Point, this island would give us over the Gulf of Mexico, and the countries and isthmus bordering on it, as well as all those whose waters flow into it, would fill up the measure of our political well-being.... Could we induce her to join us in granting its independence against all the world?"

In a prologue to the 1949 edition of *The Kingdom of This World*, Alejo Carpentier describes how during a trip to Haiti, he found himself in daily contact with something he called the *real maravilloso*, or the real marvelous.

"I was treading earth where thousands of men eager for liberty believed," he wrote. "I entered the Laferrière citadel, a structure without architectonic antecedents.... I breathed the atmosphere created by Henri Christophe, monarch of incredible undertakings.... With each step I found the real marvelous."

The real marvelous, which we have come to know as magic realism, lives and thrives in past and present Haiti, just as Haiti's revolution does. The real marvelous is in the extraordinary and the mundane, the beautiful and the repulsive, the spoken and the unspoken. It is in the enslaved African princes who believed they could fly and knew the paths of the clouds and the language of the forests but could no longer recognize themselves in the so-called New World. It is in the elaborate *vèvès*, or cornmeal drawings, sketched in the soil at Vodou ceremonies to draw attention from the gods. It is in the thunderous response from gods such as Ogoun, the god of war, who speak in the hearts of men and women who, in spite of their slim odds, accept nothing less than total freedom.

Whenever possible, Haitians cite their historical and spiritual connection to this heroic heritage by invoking the names of one or all of the founders of the country: Toussaint L'Ouverture, Henri Christophe, and Jean-Jacques Dessalines.

(The latter's fighting creed was *Koupe tèt, boule kay*—Cut heads, burn houses.)

"They can't do this to us," we say when feeling subjugated. "We are the children of Toussaint L'Ouverture, Henri Christophe, and Jean-Jacques Dessalines."

As President Aristide's opportune evocation of Toussaint L'Ouverture shows, for many of us, it is as though the Haitian revolution was fought less than two hundred days, rather than more than two hundred years, ago. For is there anything more timely and timeless than a public battle to control one's destiny, a communal crusade for self-determination?

The outcome, when it's finally achieved, can be nearly impossible to describe. It certainly was for one Haitian poet, Boisrond Tonnerre, who was given the Jeffersonian task of drafting Haiti's declaration of independence. To do it appropriately, he declared, he would need the skin of a white man for parchment, the man's skull for an inkwell, his blood for ink, and a bayonet for a pen.

At the August 1791 Vodou ceremony that would launch the more than decade-long fight for independence, the god of war Ogoun was summoned in song and a pig was sacrificed in Ogoun's honor.

"The machete suddenly buried itself in the belly of a black pig, which spewed forth guts and lungs in three squeals," Alejo Carpentier writes in *The Kingdom of This World*.

> Then, called by the name of their masters, for they had no other, the delegates came forward one by one to smear their lips with the foaming blood of the pig, caught in a wooden bowl. . . . The general staff of the insurrection had been named. . . . And in view

of the fact that a proclamation had to be drawn up and nobody knew how to write, someone remembered the goose quill of the Abbé de la Haye, priest of Dondon, an admirer of Voltaire who had shown signs of unequivocal sympathy for the Negroes ever since he had read the Declaration of the Rights of Man.

Would the Abbé lend a hand and a pen? was the burning question.

Eventually, a proclamation was drawn up and a revolution was launched, with or without the Abbé's goose quill.

CHAPTER 8

Another Country

The sea was walking the earth with a heavy heel.... The folks in the quarters and the people in the big houses further around the shore heard the big lake and wondered. The people felt uncomfortable but safe because there were the seawalls to chain the senseless monster in his bed. The folks let the people do the thinking. If the castles thought themselves secure, the cabins needn't worry.

—Zora Neale Hurston, *Their Eyes Were Watching God*

In Zora Neale Hurston's visionary 1937 novel, Janie Crawford and her boyfriend, Tea Cake, a day laborer, refuse to evacuate their small, unsteady house before a deadly hurricane batters the Florida Everglades, near where I currently live.

"Everybody was talking about it that night. But nobody was worried," wrote Hurston. "You couldn't have a hurricane when you're making seven and eight dollars a day."

It turns out you could have a hurricane, and other disasters too, even if you're making considerably less than that. And if you manage to survive that hurricane, you might end up with nothing at all. No home. No food or water. No medical care for your sick and wounded. Not even body bags or coffins for your dead.

Americans have experienced this scenario before. Not just in prophetic literature or apocalyptic blockbuster movies, but through the very real natural disasters that have plagued other countries. Catastrophes that are eventually reduced to single, shorthand images that, if necessary, can later be evoked. Take, for example, visions of skyscraper-size waves washing away entire crowds in Thailand and other Asian countries devastated by the December 2004 tsunamis. Or remember Sophia Pedro, the Mozambican woman who in March 2000 was plucked by a South African military helicopter from the tree where she had clung for three days and then given birth as the floodwaters swirled beneath her? And let's not forget Haiti's September 2004 encounter with Tropical Storm Jeanne, which left three thousand people dead and a quarter million homeless. In that disaster, patients drowned in hospital beds. Children watched as parents were washed away. Survivors sought shelter in trees and on rooftops while corpses floated in the muddy, contaminated waters around them.

As I watched all this unfold again on my television set, this time in the streets of New Orleans in the summer of 2005, I couldn't help but think of the Bush administration's initial response to the Haitian victims of Tropical Storm Jeanne the year before Hurricane Katrina struck New Orleans: sixty thousand dollars in aid and the repatriation of Haitian refugees from the United States back to the devastated region even before the waters had subsided. New Orleans' horrific tragedy had been foreshadowed in America's so-called backyard, and the initial response had been: "Po' man ain't got no business at de show," as Zora Neale Hurston's Tea Cake might have put it.

In the weeks that followed Hurricane Katrina's landing, I, immigrant writer and southern coastal city resident, heard many Americans of all geographical persuasions, pundits and citizens alike, make the case that the types of horrors that plagued Katrina-ravaged New Orleans—the desperation of ordinary citizens, some of whom resorted to raiding stores to feed themselves and their families; the forgotten public hospitals where nurses pumped oxygen into dying patients by hand; the makeshift triage wards on bridges and airports; the roaming armed gangs—are more in line with our expectations of the "third world" than the first.

Turning to the Kenyan CNN correspondent Jeff Koinange on *American Morning* a week after Hurricane Katrina struck New Orleans, the anchorwoman Soledad O'Brien said, "You know, to some degree, when you were watching the original pictures . . . if you turned the sound down on your television, if you didn't know where you were, you might think it was Haiti or maybe one of those African countries, many of which you cover."

"Watching helpless New Orleans suffering day by day left people everywhere stunned and angry and in ever greater pain," echoed *Time* magazine's Nancy Gibbs. "These things happened in Haiti, they said, but not here."

Not to be outdone, even the Canadians got in on the act. Chiding her fellow citizens for their self-righteous attitude toward American poverty, Kate Heartfield of the *Ottawa Citizen* nevertheless added, "Ottawa is not New Orleans. And it is definitely not Freetown or Port-au-Prince."

It's hard for those of us who are from places like Freetown or Port-au-Prince, and those of us who are immigrants who still have relatives living in places like Freetown or Port-au-Prince, not to wonder why the so-called developed world needs so desperately to distance itself from us, especially at times when an unimaginable disaster shows exactly how much alike we are. The rest of the world's poor do not expect much from their governments and they're usually not disappointed. The poor in the richest country in the world, however, should not be poor at all. They should not even exist. Maybe that's why both their leaders and a large number of their fellow citizens don't even realize that they actually do exist.

This is not the America we know, chimed many field reporters who, haunted by the faces and voices of the dying, the stench of bloated corpses on city streets during the day and screams for help rising from attics at night, recorded the early absence of first responders with both sorrow and rage. Their fury could only magnify ours, for if they could make it to New Orleans, Mississippi, and Alabama and give us minute-by-minute accounts of the storm and its aftermath, why couldn't the government agencies find their way there? Indeed, what these early charged news reports offered was a passport to an America where one does not always have bus fare, much less an automobile, where health insurance is as distant a dream as a college education, where poverty is a birthright, not an accident of fortune. This is the America that continues to startle, the America of the needy and never-have-enoughs, the America of the undocumented, the unemployed and underemployed, the elderly, and the infirm. An America that remains invisible until a rebellion breaks out, gunshots ring out, or a flood rages through. Perhaps this America does have more in common with the developing world than with the one it inhabits. For the poor and outcast everywhere dwell within their own country, where more often than not they must fend for themselves. That's why one can so easily become a refugee within one's own borders—because one's perceived usefulness and precarious citizenship are always in question, whether in Haiti or in that other America, the one where people have no flood insurance.

I don't know why it seems always to surprise some Americans that many of their fellow citizens are vulnerable to horrors that routinely plague much of the world's population. After all, we do share a planet whose climate is gradually being altered by unbalanced exploration and dismal environmental policies that may one day render us all, first world and third world residents alike, helpless in the face of more disasters like Tropical Storm Jeanne and Hurricane Katrina. Let us also not forget the ever-looming menace of 9/11-like terrorism, which can potentially have the same effect, landing thousands on street corners and in Astrodomes asking themselves how they came to be there.

The poor and displaced are indeed sometimes better off in places far from their impoverished homes. But in the end, must poverty also force us to live deprived of homestead, birthplace, history, memory? In the case of Hurricane Katrina, was it really a flood that washed away that nuanced privilege of deciding where one should build one's life, or was this right slowly being stripped away while we were already too horrified to watch?

One of the advantages of being an immigrant is that two very different countries are forced to merge within you. The language you were born speaking and the one you will probably die speaking have no choice but to find a common place in your brain and regularly merge there. So too with catastrophes and disasters, which inevitably force you to rethink facile allegiances.

Shortly after the terrorist attacks of September 11, 2001, Masood Farivar, a former Afghan mujahideen who received part of his education in a madrassa in Pakistan, wrote, "As an Afghan, I'd never carried the black, red, and green flag of my own country. Suddenly though, I wanted to feel what it was like to proudly hold a flag, wave it at passing ambulances, police cars, and fire trucks. It would be a good way to show my solidarity with Americans. It was my way of saying, we're in this together. I'm with you. I share your pain."

"I come from the so-called Third World," wrote the Chilean novelist and memoirist Isabel Allende after September 11, 2001, a day that also marked the twenty-eighth anniversary of a U.S.-sponsored coup d'état against her uncle, Salvador Allende. Still, she writes,

> Until only a short time ago, if someone had asked me where I'm from, I would have answered, without much thought, Nowhere; or, Latin America; or, maybe, In my heart I'm Chilean. Today, however, I say I'm an American, not simply because that's what my passport verifies, or because that word includes all of America from north to south, or because my husband, my son, my grandchildren, most of my friends, my books, and my home are in northern California; but because a terrorist attack

destroyed the twin towers of the World Trade Center, and starting with that instant, many things have changed. We can't be neutral in moments of crisis. . . . I no longer feel that I am an alien in the United States.

After the horrible carnage of September 11th, hadn't the world echoed Farivar's and Allende's sentiments and also declared, through many headlines in newspapers across the globe, that we were all Americans?

At least for a while.

Among the many realities brought to light by Hurricane Katrina was that never again could we justifiably deny the existence of this country within a country, that other America, which America's immigrants and the rest of the world may know much more intimately than many Americans do, the America that is always on the brink of humanitarian and ecological disaster. No, it is not Haiti or Mozambique or Bangladesh, but it might as well be.

CHAPTER 9

Flying Home

I used to have a fear of flying. No, I was never the hyperventilating kind of airline passenger, or the person who wouldn't even get in the air at all. But each time I was set to board an airplane, I would stay up the night before, putting my life in order, arranging important papers, cleaning my apartment. In case "the worst" ever did happen, I told myself, I wouldn't want my loved ones to have to sort through my dirty laundry—literal and otherwise—to wash my soiled dishes and pick up my cluttered piles of books off the floor. Besides, my sleepless nights always gifted me with what seemed like a shorter trip, since I would fall asleep soon after buckling my seatbelt and wouldn't wake up again until I reached my destination.

This strategy worked fine for a while, until I had to travel regularly on book-related trips. My travels then increased in frequency from my four or five yearly journeys to Haiti to stretches of two to three weeks when I would be on a different airplane once, and sometimes twice, a day.

How to make those long flights bearable? I certainly couldn't stay up every night if I were to be in half-decent shape for my book-related event the next day. So I decided to approach my plane rides in an entirely different manner; I was not going to dread them, but welcome them, value them as pockets of life experiences that couldn't take place anywhere else. I would fully embrace the "magic" of being suspended in midair, between hard ground and sky, simply like a bird, or like the jailbird Daedalus who, with his son Icarus, had crafted wings of wax and feathers to escape their earthly prisons.

I began my effort at improving my flight experiences by reading purposefully during my flights. My airplane reading would often be centered on themes. On some flights I would read only newspapers and magazines, catching up on one particular event. On other flights I would read a short novel, and finishing the entire book during the flight would give me a great thrill, as if I'd just flown a cross-Atlantic mission with Amelia Earhart.

When not reading books, I would read people, some of whom march onto planes with their life stories literally on their sleeves: a honeymooning couple sharing a heart-wrenching good-bye before being separated by a few short rows, an unaccompanied minor sobbing while ending a custodial visit with one parent to return to the other. This would make me think of Assotto Saint, a Haitian American poet and performance artist, who pegged as one of the defining moments in his life the hours he spent in the skies as a fourteen-year-old boy about to be reunited with a mother he hadn't seen for almost a decade. Of that particular plane ride, he would later write, "i wanted to write a happy carefree poem / for my childhood / lost too fast . . . / somewhere in the air / between port-au-prince & new york city / but I'm left bereft."

I too am left bereft when random acts of kindness manifest themselves in airplane aisles. Once on a flight from Port-au-Prince to Miami, a muscular white man with an elaborately tattooed arm willingly surrendered his aisle seat for a tighter middle seat so that a nervous Haitian father could sit next to his young daughter. Another time, an old woman who had trouble walking to her seat after the airline wheelchair had delivered her to the plane door was taken in the arms of a younger man and carried gently to her spot.

Once on an early morning flight from San Francisco to Miami, a woman sitting two rows behind me suffered a heart attack. I was dozing off with the shutters pulled down and a blanket over my head when a voice came over the loudspeaker asking if there was a physician onboard. It turned out there were a few, among them an affable man with salt-and-pepper hair, who immediately took control of the situation, operating an EKG machine and defibrillator from the plane's advanced first-aid kit while calmly probing the woman's distressed husband and teenage son for details of her medical history.

During the moments it took for the doctor to decide whether or not we should land so the woman could be rushed to the nearest hospital in the nearest city, her name and age and overall condition were shouted down the aisle from the doctor to the flight attendant, who was in touch with the pilot by phone.

The woman's name was Donna. She was forty-seven years old and very thin. Not at all the kind of person one might expect to be having a heart attack. Her husband explained to the doctor that she had been under some pressure at work and had brushed off three days of chest pains as symptoms of something else. At the doctor's recommendation, the pilot decided to land.

As we descended toward the snow-capped mountains of Salt Lake City, nearby passengers vacated their seats so Donna could lie down. A few even joined the flight attendants in the quick collection of cups and cans that was crucial to the last-minute landing. Community, like family, is sometimes a result of arbitrary grouping. Having ignored one another during the flight, my seatmates and I looked at one another and exchanged a few knowing nods and glances for the first time. Because suddenly we were a kind of village in the air and one of our own was in danger.

When the plane landed and the paramedics boarded to pick up Donna, one of them joked, as he made his way down the aisle, that we would not be charged for the extra stop in beautiful Salt Lake. No one laughed. Instead, as Donna was carried off the plane, many of the other passengers squeezed her son's and husband's hands and told them that they would pray for her. While we waited to take off again, I could hear snatches of conversations on cell phones and the words, "sorry," "thank you," "I love you."

My favorite flights depart late in the afternoon or early in the evening. While on those flights, I always imagine what the plane must look like to a very small child from the ground, a silvered speck racing across a flaming orange sky, nurturing the child's own dreams of escape, like they once did Assoto Saint's and countless others. I am now inside that giant sunset-framed bird and as I approach my destination I am lowered into a picture-postcard view of all the places that are lit in my arrival city, what combat fighters once called a "God's-eye view" of the luminescent ground.

Now and then on early morning flights I ask for a window seat, if there is one, in the very last row. I take off my shoes and surrender to the vibration of the engines beneath me, which produce a loud but soothing white noise. While staring out the window at the early predawn sky, I sometimes have waking dreams and watch mirages emerge from the dense high-level clouds. One morning I thought I saw Tante Ilyana—who had never been on an airplane—walking slowly over the clouds toward me. Another time I thought I spotted my childhood friend Marie Maude Gédéon, who had died of renal cancer at age thirty, joyfully doing somersaults in the celestial mist wearing the wedding dress in which she'd been buried because she was unmarried when she died.

My dread of flying returned when I was in what felt to me like a near crash between Miami and New York one summer night. As we were approaching New York's LaGuardia Airport, the plane began to nose dive as though it were being sucked down by a centrifugal force. I was looking out the window and suddenly the buildings beneath us began to blur. As the plane rattled from side to side, people screamed, some shouting for help, others calling loved ones' names, and still others shouting directly to God. Finally, the runway appeared and the plane's wheels seemed to tap the ground once, then twice, then three times, bouncing like a giant basketball. Then the plane shot back up in the air.

Everyone sat stunned into complete silence, as we waited for the captain to explain what had happened.

Finally he spoke.

"Folks, there's nothing wrong with the aircraft," he soberly declared. As we were circling the city that it seemed we had nearly crashed into, the captain assured us that we had "only" been caught in a wind shear, an aggressive type of turbulence caused by an abrupt shift in the wind's direction.

On September 10, 2001, I was on a plane with my mother, returning from a ten-day trip to Japan. My second book, a collection of short stories titled *Krik? Krak!*, had just been published there, and I had been invited to give a series of talks jointly sponsored by the American and Haitian embassies of Japan. The trip had gone quite well. In addition to work, my mother and I had done a lot of sightseeing, including at the world-famous Peace Memorial Museum in Hiroshima. On the flight back to the United States, however, I had been anxious to get home. Home being my first apartment in New Rochelle, New York, what I called my artist colony of one, in a town that had taught me the true value of writerly solitude, a town where I knew no one. The flight from Tokyo was long but uneventful. My mother read and reread the twenty-third psalm. (The LORD is my shepherd; I shall not want.) Every now and then she stopped and marveled at how much we were fed, even in coach. I made her walk every other hour to avoid blood clots in her leg.

We landed in Chicago and after a brief layover changed planes there. My themed reading for both flights was Wole Soyinka, anything I had not yet read by the Nigerian novelist, memoirist, poet, and playwright. Because New York City was our final destination, I lingered over a poem of his titled "New York, U.S.A.," which had been published more than a decade earlier.

> Control was wrested from your pilot's hands,
> And yours, mid-Atlantic, hapless voyager.
> Deafened the engine's last descent
> To all but disordered echoes of your feet.

An evening thunderstorm forced us to circle over the city for some time, making us land later in the evening than we should have. I spent a sleepless, jetlagged night at my parents' house and the next morning around seven a.m. I drove my tiny Toyota Echo to New Rochelle. Traffic was light. A better driver now, I drove assuredly, routinely, over the Whitestone Bridge and into the tree-lined streets of New Rochelle, where people were heading out for work. Then I walked into my sparsely furnished apartment, crawled onto my mattress on the floor, and fell into a deep sleep.

When I woke up a few hours later, I turned on the television hoping to catch my midday soap opera, but my television was not working. There was only television "snow," a sign that my signal had been lost. Later I would learn that it was because the tower that sent this signal to my home had been destroyed when the first plane hit the World Trade Center at 8:45 a.m. I did not have cable and, knowing nothing of what had happened, I went back to sleep. I woke up at 2:00 p.m. when my phone rang. My father had been trying to reach me, but phones were also down.

"The World Trade Center has been attacked," he said. "The towers don't exist anymore. Thousands of people have died."

I wanted to rush home, to my parents' house, but the Whitestone Bridge was closed and no trains were running. I would have to process this horrifying news for long empty hours by myself, with no one I loved within physical reach. I was alone and my writer seeking solitude was of no use. A friend's wife, who had escaped from the second tower, had temporarily gone mute from shock. My pregnant cousin had walked home to Brooklyn from midtown Manhattan, barefoot. My brother Karl, who worked near Grand Central Station, was still unaccounted for. Still, I didn't think I knew anyone who'd died in the towers, or in Pennsylvania, or in Washington? Or did I?

The next day, when I was finally able to leave New Rochelle, I took the train to Manhattan, a darker, quieter city, with MISSING flyers on subway walls and makeshift memorials on street corners. My friends and family now accounted for, I still couldn't help but feel that someday I may not be so lucky, that I may be among those wandering the streets, asking myself, the way I would nearly a decade later, during another catastrophic event in Haiti, how others could be eating and sleeping, and not be looking for a father or a mother, a son or a daughter, a husband or wife. I also felt guilty for having slept through what for so many people and their loved ones had indeed been the end of the world. That so many others would never again wake up haunted me. I felt useless and at a loss for words. "i have not written one word," the Palestinian American poet Suheir Hammad, wrote soon after September 11th, "no poetry in the ashes south of canal street."

One of the people in the ashes south of Canal Street was Michael Richards, a U.S.-born sculptor of Jamaican ancestry who had created a bronze cast statue of himself dressed as an African American World War II combat pilot, a Tuskegee airman, with dozens of miniature airplanes shooting through his body. Richards had a studio on the ninety-second floor of Tower One of the World Trade Center and was there when the first plane struck the building at 8:45 a.m. He had spent the night working on, among other things, a piece showing a man clinging to a meteor as it plunges from the sky. Richards had been interested in aviation and flight and had used them as motifs in his work for many years.

I did not know Michael Richards, but being both terrified and intrigued by the folklore of flight, I admired his work, which sometimes seemed like visual depictions of characters in pieces of literature that I loved. His pierced Tuskegee airman reminded me of Toni Morrison's flying insurance salesman in *Song of Solomon*, who wrote what must be one of the most eloquent farewell notes in the world, ending with "On Wednesday the 18th of February, 1931, I will take off from Mercy and fly away on my own wings. Please forgive me, I loved you all."

Michael Richards's *Are You Down*, a series of life-size sculptures of three fallen Tuskegee airmen, remind me of Ralph Ellison's short story "Flying Home," in which a young pilot crashes his plane and hurts himself, forcing him to ponder a lifelong love affair with airplanes. *Winged* shows two joined arms with feathers attached to them. Those arms too were Michael Richards's, cast in bronze and eerily reminiscent of the men and women jumping from the towers on September 11th, with their arms flapping as though they were trying to fly.

Did Michael Richards know *how* he was going to die? Did he somehow sense that his own body would one day represent that of so many? Maybe he was clairvoyant, what some might call "double-sighted." One can't help but hope that like the old Africans, suddenly remembering that he had the gift of flight and seeing the airplanes heading for him, he stepped out of his earthly body and flew away. In any case, he surely must have known what we all instinctively know, that we must all die and that whenever it is we die, it is always a day, a week, a month, a year, a lifetime too soon.

"The poet turns the world to glass, and shows us all things in their right series and procession," Ralph Waldo Emerson wrote. "For through that better perception he stands one step nearer to things, and sees the flowing or metamorphosis ... that within every creature is a force impelling it to ascend into a higher form."

Michael Richards was a poet of bronze and stone. He was the sculptor of private spaces and public gardens, except his gardens were purposely filled with tar and ashes. His death was no more tragic than that of the nearly three thousand other people who also left behind fingerprints on half-filled glasses and lipstick traces on collars and strands of hair on brushes and combs, but he leaves behind something that speaks not only for himself but also for them too.

"He rose one day according to his habit, before the dawn, and saw the morning break, grand as the eternity out of which it came," Emerson wrote of a sculptor from his youth, "and for many days after, he strove to express this tranquility, and lo! his chisel had fashioned out of marble the plan of a beautiful youth."

Emerson's sculptor had extracted youth from marble. Michael Richards had repeatedly chiseled himself as a dying man in agony, in pain. He had linked the European warrior Sebastian to the cunning southern African American trickster Tar Baby, titling his representation of his airplane-pierced body *Tar Baby vs. Saint Sebastian*. He had sculpted not one but two of his *Tar Baby vs. Saint Sebastian* statues, one that perished with him in the towers, and a second that was stored and then rediscovered in a cousin's garage.

Michael Richards was born in New York City, but grew up in Kingston, Jamaica, and then returned to New York as a young man, making him an American who was often called an immigrant. In Richards's obituary in *The Independent*, the art critic Adrian Dannat wrote, "Richards had gone against the expectations of his Jamaican family in becoming an artist, an extremely rare profession in a society dominated by bourgeois conventions of financial success." His friend, the art curator Moukhtar Kocache, told the *Village Voice* that Richards's work featured "men who were alienated and unacknowledged, using that for his own existential feelings as a black man, an artist, an immigrant."

"The highest minds of the world have never ceased to explore the double meaning, or shall I say quadruple or the centuple or much more manifold meaning, of every sensual fact," Emerson wrote in his essay "The Poet." "For we are not pawns and barrows, nor even porters of the fire and torch bearers, but children of the fire, made of it."

Michael Richards was a child of the fire. He often remade himself in it, using his body, over and over again, as his template.

In Ralph Ellison's "Flying Home," an old man asks Todd, the fallen young pilot, "Son, how come you want to fly way up there in the air?"

"Because," Todd replies, " . . . It's as good a way to fight and die as I know."

This leads Todd to think about a time in his childhood when he would chase the shadows of passing airplanes, thinking he could somehow capture and own them. Even the fact that the planes were being used to dump hateful and racist flyers did not diminish his admiration.

"Above he saw the plane spiraling gracefully, agleam in the sun like a fiery sword. And seeing it soar he was caught, transfixed between a terrible horror and a horrible fascination," wrote Ellison.

Unable to accept the swift reality of sudden death, I'd like to think that Michael Richards had a final moment when he was downright enthralled and mesmerized by his—our—horrible fascination. Or that maybe he had enough time to stop and whisper, "I will take off . . . and fly away on my own wings. Please forgive me, I loved you all."

Welcoming Ghosts

It was a testy interview and part of it still lives on in cyber-space via a clip on YouTube. The art historian Marc Miller asks the twenty-one-year-old graffiti artist, painter, musician, and one-time film star Jean-Michel Basquiat about his roots.

"You're what?" demands Miller. "Haitian–Puerto Rican?"

"I was born here," answers Basquiat, "but my mother's fourth-generation Puerto Rican. My father comes from Haiti."

"Do you feel that that's in your art?" continues Miller.

"Genetically?" Basquiat interrupts.

"Yeah," replies Miller. "Genetically or culturally?"

"Culturally?" Basquiat wonders out loud, almost as if speaking to himself. "I guess so."

"Haiti's of course famous for its art," Miller adds.

"That's why I said genetically," Basquiat replies while fidgeting and looking away, "because I've never been there. And I grew up in, you know, principal American vacuum. Television mostly."

"No Haitian primitives on your wall?" asks Miller.

"At home?" asks Basquiat, picking up a trace of Miller's sarcasm and running with it. "Haitian primitives? What do you mean? People? People nailed up on my walls?"

"I mean paintings," Miller answers, chuckling. "Paintings."

"No, no no," counters Basquiat. "Just, you know, typical prints you find in any home in America. Well, some homes in America. Nothing really special."

If young Basquiat had had any Haitian primitives on his walls—paintings or otherwise—one of them may have been the Haitian painter and Vodou priest Hector Hyppolite, a spiritual forebear.

Legend has it that when Hector Hyppolite was a young man, a spirit came to him in his sleep and told him that one day he would become a famous artist. Born into a family of Vodou priests, Hyppolite was no stranger to the spirits nor they to him. While waiting for this prophecy to materialize, Hyppolite traveled to Cuba to work in the sugarcane fields, then went as far as Ethiopia on a freighter, and later, when he returned to Haiti, apprenticed himself to a shoemaker, painted Vodou temples, houses, and furniture, and sketched colorful postcards that he sold to occupying U.S. marines and then painted the barroom door that would eventually change his life.

In 1943, the American watercolorist Dewitt Peters was driving through the tourist-friendly village of Montrouis with his friend the Haitian novelist Philippe Thoby-Marcelin when they spotted the colorfully painted birds and flowers on the "Ici la Renaissance" saloon door. Peters was about to open an art school and gallery (Le Centre d'Art) in downtown Port-au-Prince and was on the lookout for such talent. Enter Hector Hyppolite, who was offered the opportunity to move to a middle-class neighborhood in Port-au-Prince to concentrate solely on his art, but instead chose to settle in a seaside slum called Trou de Cochon (Pig's Hole), where he ran a Vodou temple and a boat-building business and in three years produced more than six hundred canvases.

Hyppolite's early fans and collectors were legend. André Breton, the father of French Surrealism, declared that Hyppolite could revolutionize modern art. The Tony Award–winning dancer and choreographer Geoffrey Holder created a ballet inspired by Hyppolite's life, which the Alvin Ailey Dance Company still performs. A young Truman Capote, in a December 1948 *Harper's Bazaar* magazine article, lavished praise on Hyppolite's work even while calling the artist ugly and "monkey-thin."

Hyppolite's looks fared a lot better with the American art collector Selden Rodman, who worked alongside Dewitt Peters and saw Hyppolite often at the Centre d'Art. Rodman could also have been describing young Basquiat when he wrote of Hyppolite, "His wiry hair parted in the middle and shaved around the ears, flared sidewise untrimmed with the effect of a dusty, magnetized crown.... [C]ould he be descended from one of those Arawak sand painters who inspired the vèvè?"

The *vèvè* is a ceremonial drawing, an outlined emblem that is meant to call forth spirits. It is often sketched on the ground, with ashes or cornmeal, before Vodou ceremonies. Each Vodou spirit or *lwa*—spelled *loa* in older texts—is identified with a particular *vèvè*. The *vèvè* of the goddess of love, Erzulie Freda, is usually a heart. The *vèvè* for Baron Samedi, the guardian of the cemetery, is a cross on top of a tombstone. Ogoun, the god of war, is represented by linked squares, which suggest a protective shield. Legba, master of the crossroads, is a crossroad with singularly embellished direction markers. The *vèvè* sketches are usually transient—they vanish underfoot at the ceremonies—except when sewn on sequined ceremonial flags that have stepped so far out of their ritual realm that they are now used on trendy designer purses and clothes. Like some of Hyppolite's early work, a few of Jean-Michel Basquiat's drawings and paintings bring to mind *vèvès*.

Born in Brooklyn, New York, twelve years after Hyppolite's death, Basquiat's childhood could not have been more different from Hyppolite's. Hyppolite was born dirt poor in a rural section of Haiti. Basquiat was born into a middle-class immigrant family in urban America. Where Hyppolite's exposure to art was mostly limited to the practical and decorative—brightly painted houses, Vodou temples, Masonic lodges, boats, and camions called tap taps—Basquiat often visited museums with his mother and, if Julian Schnabel's biopic of Basquiat is to be believed, young Basquiat saw his mother cry before Pablo Picasso's *Guernica* while a golden crown appeared halo-like on his head. Basquiat had his own pass to the Brooklyn Museum at a very young age and was a visual vampire. Bored and haunted, he left home as a teenager and lived on the streets of Manhattan, where he began taking hard drugs and painting cryptic phrases on downtown walls.

Like Hyppolite, Basquiat was extraordinarily prolific during his short career, and before settling primarily on canvas both men used all types of tools and surfaces from spray paint (Basquiat) to chicken feathers (Hyppolite), doors (both Basquiat and Hyppolite), bed frames (Hyppolite), helmets (Basquiat), and mattresses (Basquiat). Whether any mystical dreams had led him to that conclusion we don't know, but a teenage Basquiat had announced to his Haitian father that he would be "very, very famous one day."

Because he was a lifelong *sèvitè*, a devotee of Vodou, an older and more mature Hector Hyppolite—who was forty-nine years old when he was "discovered"—saw his art as a gift from the *lwas* and carefully tried to balance its demands and rewards. The canvas, for Hyppolite, was just one more space in which to serve the *lwas*, and when he served them properly they rewarded him with ideas for paintings.

Later, as his career flourished, Hyppolite would continually consult with the spirits, requesting their consent to remain an artist, especially as his hectic engagement with his art began to leave less time for his work as a Vodou priest, or *hougan* (spelled *ougan* in today's Creole).

"I haven't practiced vaudou [an alternative spelling of Vodou] for a while," he told Selden Rodman, during one of the collector's visits to the artist's dirt-floored, palm-frond shack. "I asked the spirits' permission to suspend my work as a hougan, because of my painting. . . . The spirits agreed that I should stop for a while. I've always been a priest, just like my father and my grandfather, but now I am more an artist than a priest."

In a collective religion like Vodou, Maya Deren wrote in *Divine Horsemen: The Living Gods of Haiti*, "to create a physical statement (whether a painting or a drum beat) . . . would require an individual at once saint and artistic genius."

Why?

Because, wrote Deren, "virtuoso is the province of divinity. Only the loa are virtuosi."

Also believing this, even though he was possibly the most famous Haitian artist of his time, Hector Hyppolite painted as though he were what Maya Deren labeled an anonymous inventor, a member of a collective run by the gods.

Though he didn't always cite the island nation as a direct influence, Basquiat was certainly aware of, if not Hyppolite, certainly Haiti. Basquiat was perhaps asked about Haiti as much as he was about Puerto Rico and the continent of Africa, about which he told Demosthenes Davvetas of *New Art International*, "I've never been to Africa. I'm an artist who has been influenced by his New York environment. But I have a cultural memory. I don't need to look for it, it exists. It's over there, in Africa. That doesn't mean that I have to go live there. Our cultural memory follows us everywhere, wherever you live."

It is perhaps out of a similar cultural memory that many of Basquiat's Haiti-related paintings emerged, paintings like *Untitled 1982*, which has HAITI printed in bold letters on the canvas. Above the word HAITI is a partially masked face and Basquiat's signature crown, floating beneath the word LOANS, highlighting Haiti's massive debts and tracing the history of those debts from the conquistador Hernán Cortés to Napoleon Bonaparte, whose first name is crossed out, down to one of the leaders of the Haitian revolution, Toussaint L'Ouverture, whose name is underlined. Even Basquiat's choice of that particular spelling of L'Ouverture's self-designated last name—which is most often spelled Louverture—makes L'Ouverture a figure that is closer to Legba, the master of the crossroads, "the opening," the one through whom we enter. Near the word HAITI in the painting is the word SALT, which is, according to Haitian legend, what one gives to zombies in order to liberate them from their eternal bondage, to make them human again.

Toussaint L'Ouverture reappears with a black hat and sword in Basquiat's 1983 painting *Toussaint L'Ouverture Versus Savonarola*. Here Basquiat enrolls the Black Spartacus to battle the Italian priest and destroyer of so-called immortal art. Who wins that battle in Basquiat's mind? Perhaps one day this painting may inspire some type of avant-garde video game.

Haiti, like Puerto Rico and the continent of Africa, was obviously both in Basquiat's consciousness and in his DNA, but they were not there by themselves. Basquiat did not belong to any fixed collective. He freely borrowed from and floated among many cultural and geographic traditions. Like many other culturally mixed, first- or second-generation Americans, his collectivity was fluid. He was symbiotic and syncretic in the same way that Hector Hyppolite's Vodou paintings were, mixing European Catholicism and African religious rites and adapting them to a world made new by the artist's vision or, in both Hyppolite's and Basquiat's case, visions.

In digging deeper for a Haitian influence in Basquiat's oeuvre, one might identify as Ogoun his arrow-wielding men or as a tribute to Baron Samedi and Erzulie his heart-covered skulls and crosses. But even if this were undeniably true, even if Basquiat were, like Hyppolite, purposely drawing *vèvès* and other visual tributes to the *lwas*, he was also trying to repel ghosts, much like the sad and frightened-looking young man in the painting of that name. A young man who seems almost split in two, wearing a cross (or is it an ankh?) around his neck, while leaning on an old man's cane, like Legba, the gatekeeper, the *lwa* who mediates between the world of the spirits and the world of mortals, the god who stands at physical and spiritual intersections, the one to whom one has to say to be allowed safe passage, "Papa Legba, please make a way, open the gates for me."

The bottom half of the young man's body in *To Repel Ghosts* is claimed by an unfinished heart. Might it belong to Erzulie, the Haitian goddess of love, who often demands ritual marriage to promising men, something to which Hyppolite might have been more amiable than Basquiat? Hector Hyppolite would never think of repelling his ghosts. He welcomed them. They had chosen him, inspired him. They had nurtured his art. Maybe they'd done the same for Basquiat, but something may have been lost in the translation and Basquiat may not have been able to recognize or understand them.

Basquiat died of a drug overdose in 1988 at age twenty-seven. Perhaps if he had lived, he would have learned to embrace these types of ghosts, among his many others. We never got to see, for example, how Basquiat's brief and much-anticipated trip to the Ivory Coast might have affected his work. He might have altered his style a bit (or not) or he might have changed directions completely, becoming the poet he'd told friends he wanted to be. Hyppolite too might have changed styles or direction had he not died of a heart attack in 1948 at age fifty-four. Who knows where the spirits might have led them both? Or maybe they had fulfilled their missions and had nothing more to do or say, or create.

In Vodou, it is believed that when one dies, one returns to Ginen, the ancestral homeland from which our forebears were taken before being brought to the New World as slaves. Ginen stands in for all of Africa, renaming with the moniker of one country an ideological continent which, if it cannot welcome the returning bodies of its lost children, is more than happy to welcome back their spirits. In Vodou, it is also believed that possession, trance, is an opportunity for the spirits to speak to mortals and the person who is in trance, or possessed, becomes the vessel, the *chwal* or divine horseman or horsewoman, through whom the spirits speak. Both Basquiat and Hyppolite were in a type of trance, divine horsemen, possessed, as their hyperproductivity shows, by spirits they were seeking to either welcome or repel. Possession, however, is not supposed to last a lifetime. Neither the body nor the mind could bear or sustain it.

It may be that Basquiat knew this all too well. When Marc Miller asked him about the Haitian primitives who should have been nailed to his walls, perhaps all Basquiat could think of was the primitive in the mirror, the anonymous inventor, who was plucked from obscurity and turned into a god only to be continually called crude, naive, savage, and later even "a Madison Avenue Primitive," as he was labeled in a November 9, 1992, review by Adam Gopnik in the *New Yorker*. Gone, except in these perhaps misunderstood shapes and forms, maybe the Madison Avenue primitive is now side by side with the Trou de Cochon primitive, if not in some collector's storage space, then in their common ancestral Ginen, or possibly, in a few cheap prints nailed to some young artist's wall.

Acheiropoietos

On November 12, 1964, after Marcel Numa and Louis Drouin were executed and their bodies carried away, some say to the national palace to be personally inspected by François "Papa Doc" Duvalier, a lanky thirteen-year-old boy who had been standing in the back of the crowd to avoid the thunderous sounds of the executioner's guns, stepped forward as the spectators and soldiers scattered. He walked toward the bullet-ridden poles, bent down in the blood-soaked dirt, and picked up the eyeglasses that Louis Drouin had been wearing.

The young man, Daniel Morel, only momentarily held the eyeglasses in his hands before they were snatched away by another boy, but in the moment he had them, he'd noticed tiny chunks of Drouin's brain splattered on the cracked lenses. Perhaps if he had kept them, he might have cleaned the lenses and raised them to his face, to try to see the world the way it might have been reflected in a dead man's eyes. Often in Haiti, the eyes of murder victims are gouged out by their murderers because it is believed that even after death, the last image a person sees remains imprinted on his or her cornea, as clearly as a photograph.

Before witnessing the execution of Marcel Numa and Louis Drouin, Daniel Morel was not particularly interested in dead men's eyes. He had been like any other boy, going for long walks all over Port-au-Prince and playing soccer with his friends. He sometimes worked in his father's bakery and tried to climb aboard Haiti's commercial train, which brought sugarcane stalks from the southern fields of Léogâne to the sugar-making plant in Port-au-Prince. But the execution changed everything.

The next day, he walked by a photographer's studio near his father's bakery in downtown Port-au-Prince, and on the open paneled doors were enlarged photographs of Marcel Numa and Louis Drouin's corpses, purposely put on display as deterrents for the country's potential dissenters. These pictures were exhibited there and elsewhere for weeks and young Daniel Morel would walk past them, and even though he had been at the execution, he saw them each day as if for the first time, and was unable to look away.

"That's when I decided to be a photojournalist," Daniel recalled more than forty-five years later, while sitting at the dining room table in my home in Miami's Little Haiti neighborhood.

We had met nearly a decade earlier while I was in Haiti with some Haitian American journalist friends. It was All Saints' Day and we had all gone with him to Port-au-Prince's national cemetery to watch groups of people sing, dance, and pray inside the cemetery, to honor their dead.

No one is absolutely certain now where Numa and Drouin are buried, so I know that they were not among the dead being singled out for prayers at the national cemetery that day. From the images I had seen of the execution, I had tried while walking along the narrow corridors between the mausoleums and graves to figure out the location. I had decided that a cracked and graffiti-covered cement wall next to the main entrance might be the spot, a wall with a bustling neighborhood and a trash-filled ravine on its outer side.

I didn't know of Daniel's connection to Numa and Drouin the first time we met. And he did not know of my interest in them. In fact, we did not even speak to each other because he was busy taking photographs. I learned that he had been at the execution site only when I heard him speak at an exhibition of his photographs in New Paltz, New York, in the fall of 2006.

"I immediately wanted to be a photographer so that I could document Haitian history," he'd said that day.

Elaborating during our conversation at my house, he added, "There were no recent or useful photographs in the Haitian history books I studied from when I was a boy. As far as those books were concerned, Haitian history ended in 1957, before François Papa Doc Duvalier came to power. In photography, history is something that happened ten minutes ago. Photography documents life, movement, but it also documents history and death."

"Photography is an elegiac art," the novelist and essayist Susan Sontag writes in *On Photography*. "All photographs are *memento mori*." That is, they remind us, as Roland Barthes explains in *Camera Lucida*, that sooner or later the subject will no longer exist.

"To take a photograph," Sontag continues, "is to participate in another person's (or thing's) mortality, vulnerability, mutability. Precisely by slicing out this moment and freezing it, all photographs testify to time's relentless melt."

Daniel Morel has been trying to document Haiti's relentless melt ever since he saw Marcel Numa and Louis Drouin die. His instantly recognizable images, distributed for fifteen years by wire news services to publications all over the world, are raw and startling, urgent and frightening, like screams rising from an unending nightmare. He does not spare his subjects or his viewers any more than life would spare them. He is a witness, but barely there. You almost have a feeling that the photographs take themselves, because they document acts that you'd expect people to take part in only when others are not around: biting another's dismembered finger, setting a pile of men on fire.

Children in quiet distress—as Daniel and many of the other youngsters may have been while watching Numa and Drouin die—often appear in his oeuvre. They are carrying heavy objects, cement blocks, buckets. They are dwarfed by mountains of trash or packed in tiny classrooms. They are cradling the bloody heads of their dying friends on the street. When among the skeletal dead, they are nearly falling off the edge of crowded gurneys, a limb hanging down, as if reaching for the earth in which no one can afford to properly bury them.

During the Duvalier dictatorship, Morel, now a gray-haired and bearded soft-spoken middle-aged man, explains, no one was allowed to walk around with a camera in front of Haiti's presidential palace. If you did, you risked being mistaken for a spy and getting shot. Pictures, except when used for fright and propaganda, were taken at home or inside professional portrait studios, where people sat and posed and tried to look either pensive or satisfied. He wanted to reclaim the power of propaganda photos from the state and return it to the subjects, but he could not do that before leaving Haiti at seventeen.

His first photography assignment was in college, in Hawaii, where he photographed a cooking class. For the second, he photographed former president Jimmy Carter while Carter was visiting Hawaii. Surrounded by an army of photographers, Daniel was seduced by the clatter of all the shutters and flashes around him, what Roland Barthes calls "the living sound" of a photograph and what Daniel Morel refers to as "the klak klak klak klak" of it all.

The nonpersonal photographic images he often has in mind while working are of the death of Marcel Numa and Louis Drouin, the assassination of John F. Kennedy, and Jack Ruby's televised shooting of Lee Harvey Oswald, which he saw, as a boy, in graphic stills in the pages of *Paris Match* magazine. He would later capture similar images in his work, leading some to criticize him for his penchant for showing only the harshest, most violent side of Haitian life.

"A lot of people see my pictures," he says. "They tell me 'you make the country look bad.' People sometimes say my photos are too negative. They're shocked by them, but that's exactly the reaction I want to get from people. I am not trashing Haiti or denigrating it. I am just showing people the way things are because maybe if they see it with their own eyes, they'll do something to change the situation."

In 1980, Daniel returned to Haiti from Hawaii. He traveled across the Haitian countryside photographing country weddings and wakes. He began taking news-related photographs after the end of the Duvalier dictatorship in 1986, when the streets were filled with the corpses of the Duvaliers' former henchmen. He worked for several Haitian newspapers and took the occasional freelance assignment from foreign newspapers until he was doing most of his work for wire news services.

In 2004, after the second departure of President Jean-Bertrand Aristide and a personal tragedy in which his wife was brutally mauled to death by a guard dog, he left Haiti and moved back to the United States, where he has been struggling to make a living as a photographer. Now, as an older immigrant, he finds it much harder to rebuild his life and career.

"I have no country now," he says. "I can't live in Haiti and I can't live in the U.S. In Haiti they called me *jounalis la, atis la*, the journalist, the artist," he says, "Here, I feel like I have little value."

He does not feel sorry for himself. He has seen too many horrors for that. If anything, he would like to document this stage in his life, frame by frame, day by day.

Eight months before we met in Miami, he was beginning to lose his balance, and then fell and hit his head so hard that he cannot remember where he hit it. He suffered a concussion and some bleeding in the brain, and when he went to the hospital for an MRI, a benign tumor was found in his brain. Before he could have the surgery, he had to be given plasma and spent nineteen days in a New England hospital, and every day he photographed the daylong frost and striking winter sunrise and sunset outside his hospital room window. Sometimes a sparrow would show up in the window and peek in at him, and he would be convinced that the sparrow was the spirit of his dead wife. Though he had been unable to bring himself to photograph his wife's body after she died, he photographed the sparrow, seeing in this bird a chance to salvage some beauty out of horrible tragedy. During his stay in the hospital, he photographed the staff and all his procedures. He used overhead mirrors to photograph himself photographing himself. Before his brain surgery, he asked the surgeons to photograph his open skull and exposed brain, a picture of which he later showed me.

What was it like, I asked him, turning the camera on himself, to document his own mortality?

"I was joyful," he said. "I was happy. Even if these were my last pictures, I would have died with the camera in my hand. I have documented others. I couldn't die without documenting myself."

As he recovered from the surgery, though, he began thinking of his archive of twenty-five years' worth of pictures, each image, he was happy to discover, still imprinted on his brain, just as they'd been before the surgery. He is thinking, however, of concentrating now on other types of images.

"I'd like to take pictures with less conflict and tension, less provocative pictures," he says, "I'd like to show the beauty of Haiti because when I lived there I saw as much beauty as ugliness. I smelled as much trash as the great smell of bread baking in my father's bakery in downtown Port-au-Prince."

He is working on a book about Haiti's oldest musical group, Orchestre Septentrional d'Haiti. The band had once written and performed songs honoring François "Papa Doc" Duvalier. Perhaps they had done this as a means of survival because they'd witnessed from the stage how people were brutally beaten and sometimes even shot dead by the Duvaliers' henchmen at their shows. The musicians of Orchestre Septentrional would later write and perform songs encouraging resistance and struggle and celebrating the end of the dictatorship. Because Orchestre Septentrional d'Haiti was adored by Duvalier's Tonton Macoutes, Daniel Morel had once dismissed them, thinking that they were *mizisyen palè*, mercenary artists. But one time he had a flat tire near a club where they were performing and, while waiting for the tire to get fixed, he fell madly in love with their music without realizing it was theirs.

"In Haiti music is a big part of the political landscape," he writes, along with his collaborator Jane Regan, in the afterword to their still unpublished Septentrional book. "Each regime has had music that helped it take power. And each used music to stay in power. And music was also often used to help bring regimes down. Haitian politicians figure out which bands are the most popular and they support them—with instruments, funding for carnival and 'fêtes champêtres' (country festivals) appearances and so on.... Septentrional has so far survived the political and social storms which have ravaged Haiti the country and the musical and cultural ones which threaten to bury all that is Haitian."

He appreciates the group so much now that he's also working on a documentary film about them. When he stopped by my house in Miami, he was on his way to photograph the funeral of one of the group's oldest leaders.

"I am not going to photograph his death," he said, "I am going to photograph his life. Someone can be in a coffin and you can bring them back to life if you capture them well enough, if you capture their spirit. I don't photograph death at funerals. I photograph life."

I ask him if he thinks there's a link between photography and death, and he laughs and says, "Posing is death. I think when you make people pose for a photograph, you kill them."

I tell him about a studio photographer in Little Haiti who says that he became a photographer because his mother died when he was a baby and, since there were no photographs of her, he never got to see her face. Now this man purposely takes portraits of other people's mothers and imagines his own in them.

I also cite my favorite Haitian poem that mentions photographs, Felix Morisseau Leroy's "Tourist," and recite a few lines by heart.

> Tourist, don't take my picture
> Don't take my picture, tourist
> I'm too ugly
> Too dirty
> Too skinny
> Don't take my picture, white man
> Mr. Eastman won't be happy
> I'm too ugly
> Your camera will break
> I'm too dirty
> Too black

At the heart of this is a plea from the voice at the other end of the lens—a very rare moment when a poverty-stricken photography subject actually speaks—of the fear of being misread, mis-seen, and misunderstood, of being presented out of context. It is a fear that is very similar to that of other subjects who worried that their souls might be stolen through the narrow lenses of a machine that exists outside of their experience. Allowing one's self to be photographed, both when the photographer is a stranger and when it is someone we know, is an act of great trust. And one can sense when there is comfort and discomfort between the subject and the lens, the capturer and the captured. And captured is what many of the subjects of Daniel's pictures are. Even before their photographs were taken, they were already captured by the gods of painful circumstances.

On the flip side, though, of one person begging not to be photographed is another paradigm. Please take my picture, someone caught in an impossible situation might say.

> Jounalis la, please take my picture
> Please take my picture, atis la
> I'm needy
> Desperate
> Trapped
> Please take my picture, jounalis
> Screw Mr. Eastman
> I'm not too ugly
> Your camera will not break
> I'm not too dirty
> Not too black

After four consecutive storms ravaged Haiti, my friend the *Miami Herald* journalist Jacqueline Charles told me how, when she arrived with the photographer Patrick Farrell at a catastrophic scene where some dead children had been fished out of an overflowing river, a grieving father begged for some clean water to wash his mud-covered daughter and for a pretty dress to put on her before her photograph—which was later part of a Pulitzer Prize–winning series of photographs—was taken. Knowing that this would be the last image of his daughter, the father wanted her to look her absolute best.

The father, Jacqueline told me, desperately wanted his daughter's story to be told, knowing that though hers was a singular tale, her face a singular image, it could reveal a great deal about the larger disaster of the storms. In that way, the heartbroken father was following a long-honored tradition, in Haiti and elsewhere, of taking a keepsake photograph of the dead as a way of keeping them with us, and at the same time allowing his loved one's face to stand for many.

Another photographer, an Israeli named Daniel Kedar, had traveled all over Haiti and taken pictures of peasant farmers who'd never seen photographs of themselves. They sometimes denied their own image to him when he handed them the instantly printed photographs.

"No, I am not that skinny," some would say. "No, I am not that old."

When everything does not rely on our image, do we imagine ourselves at all? Is there even a need for it when our face is ours alone? To suddenly become emblematic of a problem, the "face" of a ravaged Haiti, is its own rude awakening, its own culture shock. Yet it allows a larger story to be told that in many ways can be helpful, because it fights complete erasure. It forces others to remember that we were—are—here.

"*Pito nou lèd, nou la*," boldly claims the Haitian proverb. Better that we are ugly, but we are here.

"Photography has something to do with resurrection," Roland Barthes wrote, "might we not say of it what the

Byzantines said of the image of Christ which impregnated St. Veronica's napkin: that it was not made by the hand of man, *acheiropoietos*?"

Might we not say the same of all impassioned creative endeavors?

"I never intended to become a photojournalist," Daniel Morel tells me more than once. "I became a photojournalist because at Numa and Drouin's execution, I felt afraid and I never wanted to feel afraid again. I take pictures so I am never afraid of anyone or anything. When I take pictures, I feel like something is shielding me, like the camera is protecting me."

Did he, as a boy, want to protect Numa and Drouin? I ask.

He could not protect them, he said, but over the years he has felt as though he's managed to protect other Numas and other Drouins with his photographs. And during this final conversation, I am even more certain that to create dangerously is also to create fearlessly, boldly embracing the public and private terrors that would silence us, then bravely moving forward even when it feels as though we are chasing or being chased by ghosts.

At the beginning of his 1955 short story "Jonas ou l'artiste au travail" (Jonah, or the Artist at Work), Albert Camus cites as an epigraph the following verse from the book of Jonah.

> Take me up and cast me forth into
> the sea . . . for I know that for my
> sake this great tempest is upon you.

Creating fearlessly, like living fearlessly, even when a great tempest is upon you. Creating fearlessly even when cast *lòt bò dlo*, across the seas. Creating fearlessly for people who see/ watch/listen/read fearlessly. Writing fearlessly because, as my friend Junot Díaz has said, "a writer is a writer because even when there is no hope, even when nothing you do shows any sign of promise, you keep writing anyway." This is perhaps also what it means to be a writer. Writing as though nothing can or will ever stop you. Writing as though you full-heartedly, or foolhardily, believe in *acheiropoietos*.

There is something about doing your own grieving in a place filled with other people's grief. The last time I was at the Port-au-Prince national cemetery was for the February 2003 burial of my Aunt Denise. At that time, as at many others, I looked around yet again at a peeling section of the cement wall against which I believed the blood of Marcel Numa and Louis Drouin had once been splattered. The story goes that the wall had been built a few decades before the execution of Marcel Numa and Louis Drouin, when a pleading female voice was heard coming from the leaves of a massive soursop tree that stood in the middle of the cemetery. The voice coming from the soursop tree was that of Gran Brigit, the wife of Baron Samedi, the guardian spirit of the cemetery. Gran Brigit was known for her generosity in granting money to the poor. So as news of Gran Brigit's manifested presence spread, massive crowds filled the cemetery, trampling the mausoleums and graves. The wall was built to keep Gran Brigit's followers out.

I looked around at this massive hamlet of the dead and wondered where Gran Brigit's tree might have stood. I stared at the old two-story building near the cemetery entrance, the balcony of which was where I believed many had stood to watch the execution of Marcel Numa and Louis Drouin. Neither the building nor the wall may be what or where I thought them to be. I tell this story now with the unreliability of that uncertainty.

On the wall that I believed had served as the background for these executions, I saw political graffiti. Aba——, Down with ———. Not the name of a Haitian national figure, but someone I did not know. The words were written in the same type of black spray-painted cursive, the ubiquitous graffiti scrawl that one still finds all over Port-au-Prince, street commentary that suggests that Haiti's capital may be full of Jean-Michel Basquiats. There was, the last time I was in the cemetery, no plaque anywhere to acknowledge what had happened there to Marcel Numa and Louis Drouin on November 12, 1964.

"If we began to put plaques all over Port-au-Prince to commemorate deaths," a friend had once told me when I'd pointed this out to him, "we would have room for little else."

In lieu of plaques, all we have of Numa and Drouin are individual memories like Daniel Morel's and a few minutes of black-and-white film in which they die over and over again and some photographs in which they remain dead.

The last time Daniel Morel was in the cemetery, there was a pile of corpses as high as the wall itself, all of them victims of the earthquake that struck Haiti on January 12, 2010. Marcel Numa and Louis Drouin's death place proved too small a burial ground for the more than two hundred thousand people who had instantly died together in Port-au-Prince that afternoon.

Daniel Morel's would be among the first pictures of death and destruction to emerge from Haiti soon after the earthquake. He happened to be visiting Port-au-Prince from the United States and was walking the streets when the earthquake struck. There was no returning now to the more "pleasant" images of a city and country that he'd been documenting since he was a boy. His—our—entire city was a cemetery.

Our Guernica

My cousin Maxo has died. The house that I called home during my visits to Haiti collapsed on top of him.

Maxo was born on November 4, 1948, after three days of agonizing labor. "I felt," my Aunt Denise used to say, "as though I spent all three days pushing him out of my eyes."

She had a long scar above her right eyebrow, where she had jabbed her nails through her skin during the most painful moments. She never gave birth again.

Maxo often complained about his parents not celebrating his birthday.

"Are you kidding me?" I'd say, taking his mother's side. "Who would want to remember such an ordeal?"

Jokes aside, it pained him more than it should have, even though few children in Bel Air, the impoverished and now devastated neighborhood where we grew up, ever had a birthday party with balloons and cake.

Maxo once told me that when he was a teenager his favorite author was Jean Genet. He read and reread *Les Nègres*. He liked all the wild language in the play, the way you could easily lose track of what was going on, not understand much of what people were doing and saying, and then suddenly feel as though each of the characters was directly addressing you. He felt it was a perfect play for Haiti, one that could easily have been written by a Haitian.

In light of Maxo's death, these lines from the play now haunt me: "Your song was very beautiful, and your sadness does me honor. I'm going to start life in a new world. If I ever return, I'll tell you what it's like there. Great black country, I bid thee farewell."

Two days after a 7.0 earthquake struck Haiti, on January 12, 2010, I was still telling my brothers that one night, as we were watching the television news, Maxo would pop up behind one of the news anchors and take over his job.

Maxo was a hustler. He could get whatever he wanted, whether money or kind words, simply by saying, "You know I love you. I love you. I love you." It worked with many of our family members in New York, both when he occasionally showed up to visit and when he called from Haiti to ask them to fund his various projects. With a voice that blended shouting and laughter, he made each of his requests for money sound as though it were an investment that the giver would be making in him- or herself.

The last time I heard from Maxo was three days before the earthquake. He left a message on my voice mail. He was trying to raise money to rebuild the small school I had visited with his son Nick and my Uncle Joseph in the mountains of Léogâne in the summer of 1999. The school had been destroyed by a mudslide a few weeks earlier. Thankfully, none of the children had been hurt. (It's interesting that both Maxo and his father had the school in mind as one of the last things each wanted to do before he died.)

When Maxo's father, my eighty-one-year-old Uncle Joseph, left Haiti in 2004, after a gang threatened his life, Maxo was with him. They traveled together to Miami, hoping to be granted political asylum. Instead, they were detained by the U.S. Department of Homeland Security and were separated while in custody. When Maxo was finally able to see his father, it was to translate for the detention center's medical staff, who accused my uncle, as he vomited both from his mouth and from a tracheotomy hole in his neck, of faking his illness. The next day my uncle died and Maxo was released from detention. It was Maxo's fifty-sixth birthday. Once the pain of his father's death had eased, he joked, "My parents never wanted me to have a happy birthday."

After his asylum petition was denied, Maxo returned to Haiti. He missed his five youngest children, some of whom were constantly calling to ask when he was coming home. There was also his father's work to continue—small schools and churches to oversee all over Haiti. The return, though, was brutal. During our telephone calls, he talked about the high price of food in Port-au-Prince. "If it's hard for me, imagine for the others," he'd say.

His time in detention in the United States had sensitized him to prison conditions and to prisoners' lack of rights in Haiti. He often called asking for money to buy food, which he then took to the national penitentiary. (The penitentiary was one of the few government buildings that remained standing after the January 2010 earthquake, though all the prisoners managed to escape.)

Maxo's generosity, along with the Haitian sense of kindness and community, is perhaps why, immediately after four stories collapsed on him on January 12th, family, friends, and even strangers began to dig for him and his wife and their children. They freed his wife and all but one of his children, ten-year-old Nozial, from the rubble two days later. Even when there was little hope, they continued to dig for Maxo and for those who had died along with him: some children who were being tutored after school, the tutors, a few parents who had stopped by to discuss their children's schoolwork. We will never know for sure how many.

The day that Maxo's remains were found, the call from Bel Air came with some degree of excitement. At least he would not rest permanently in the rubble. At least he would not go into a mass grave. Somehow, though, I sense that he would not have minded. Everyone is being robbed of rituals, he might have said. Why not me?

By the time Maxo's body was uncovered, cell phones were finally working again, bringing a flurry of voices. One cousin had an open gash in her head that was still bleeding. Another had a broken back and had been carried to three field hospitals trying to get it X-rayed. Another was sleeping outside her house and was terribly thirsty. An in-law had no blood-pressure medicine. Most had not eaten for days. There were friends and family members whose entire towns had been destroyed, and dozens from whom we have had no word at all.

Everyone sounded eerily calm on the phone. No one was screaming. No one was crying. No one said, "Why me?" or "We're cursed." Even as the aftershocks kept coming, they'd say, "The ground is shaking again," as though this had become a normal occurrence. They inquired about family members outside Haiti: an elderly relative, a baby, my one-year-old daughter.

I cried and apologized. "I'm sorry I can't be there with you," I said.

My nearly six-foot-tall twenty-three-year-old cousin—the beauty queen we nicknamed NC (Naomi Campbell)—who says that she is hungry and has been sleeping in bushes with dead bodies nearby, stops me.

"Don't cry," she says. "That's life."

"No, it's not life," I say. "Or it shouldn't be."

"It is," she insists. "That's what it is. And life, like death, lasts only *yon ti moman*." Only a little while.

I was thinking about Maxo, Nozial, NC, Tante Zi, and many others when the media called to ask for my reaction to the earthquake and its aftermath. I was numb, like everybody else, I wanted to say, tallying my losses, remembering each moment of every day, someone I had not heard from, someone I had not been able to reach. But once we got past the personal angle, shedding my reluctance to speak for the collective, this is what I felt I had to say. I said: Haitians like to tell each other that Haiti is *tè glise*, slippery ground. Even under the best of circumstances, the country can be stable one moment and crumbling the next. Haiti has never been more slippery ground than after this earthquake, with bodies littering the streets, entire communities buried in rubble, homes pancaked to dust. Now Haitian hearts are also slippery ground, hopeful one moment and filled with despair the next. Has two hundred and six years of existence finally reached its abyss? we wonder. But now even the ground is no more.

I said that our love for Haiti had not changed, that in fact it had become even deeper. But Haiti, or what is left of it, had changed. It had changed physically, earthquake fault lines catastrophically rearranging its landscape. The mountains that had been stripped of their trees, mined for charcoal and construction materials, and then crowded with unsteady homes had crumbled, leaving both the poor and the rich homeless.

This is a natural disaster, I explained, but one that had been in the making for a long time, partly owing to the complete centralization of goods and services and to the import-favoring agricultural policies that have driven so many Haitians off their ancestral lands into a capital city built for two hundred thousand that was forced to house nearly three million. If a tropical storm could bury an entire city under water as Tropical Storm Jeanne did Gonaïves in 2004, if mudslides could bring down entire neighborhoods with homes and schools and people in them, then what chance did Port-au-Prince and the surrounding area have against a 7.0 magnitude earthquake? With thousands hastily and superficially buried or lodged in miles and miles of rubble, I said, Haiti is no longer just slippery ground, but also sacred ground.

I tried to say some of this whenever I went on the radio or on television, whenever I wrote my articles of fifteen hundred words or less. They were therapeutic for me, these media outings, and helpful, I hoped, in adding one more voice to a chorus of bereavement and helping to explain what so many of us were feeling, which was a deep and paralyzing sense of loss.

Maybe that was my purpose, then, as an immigrant and a writer—to be an echo chamber, gathering and then replaying voices from both the distant and the local devastation. Still words often failed me.

"no poetry in the ashes south of canal street," the poet Suheir Hammad had written.

Would there be any poetry amidst the Haitian ruins?

It was too soon to even try to write, I told myself. You were not there. You did not live it. You have no right even to speak— for you, for them, for anyone. So I did what I always do when my own words fail me. I read.

I read hundreds of first-person narratives, testimonials, blogs. One of the most heartbreaking was written by Dolores Dominique Neptune, one of Jean Dominique's daughters, Jan J. Dominique's younger sister.

"Here is the tale of the death of Jean Olivier Neptune written by his mother Dolores Dominique Neptune," the person who forwarded it to me noted.

"Where is my son? The house collapsed. He is in his room. On his bed," Dolores Dominique Neptune wrote. "I call his name. I call on God and negotiate with Him. I call on the neighbors. What neighbors? All their houses have collapsed and no one will come."

Later, after a massive effort by many neighbors and friends who literally emerged out of the rubble to help, she found her son.

"What an angel!" she wrote. "His left hand is resting on his stomach as he lies in his bed. My son is dead!"

A few days later, I read my friend the novelist Évelyne Trouil-lot, who wrote from Port-au-Prince, in a January 20, 2010, opinion piece for the *New York Times*, "The family has set up camp in my brother's house. I live just next door, but it makes us feel better to be all in the same house. My brother, a novelist, is writing his articles; I am writing mine."

I read her brother, the novelist Lyonel Trouillot, who was posting daily accounts of life after the quake on the Web site of the French publication *Le Point*.

"Last night," he wrote on day five, "I heard the drums from a Vodou ceremony. I didn't have enough energy to go and find out if they were praising or rebuking the gods. I started heading there anyway, but came across a group of people playing dominoes by moonlight. I listened to the jokes being told by the players, about both the living and the dead. . . . I know that like them, at the end of the day, both to forget the darkness and to not curse the dawn, I need to laugh."

I too needed to laugh, so I began reading my friend Dany Laferrière again. Dany is one of the funniest people I know and his sense of humor often infuses his work. Dany was, along with Lyonel and Évelyne Trouillot, one of the writer organizers of a literary festival called Étonnants Voyageurs, which was to have started in Port-au-Prince on January 14, 2010. Some health concerns regarding my one-year-old daughter had forced me to turn down the invitation to participate in the festival. Given that I often travel to Haiti with my family and that we often try to add a few days at the beginning or the end of trips like these, it is possible that if we had agreed to attend Étonnants Voyageurs, we, along with forty other writers who live outside of Haiti, might have been either additional victims or survivors of the earthquake.

Dany Laferrière was an additional survivor of the earthquake. A few days later, he returned to Canada, where he lives, to tell of what he had seen: of the bravery and dignity of Haitians who initially received no outside help and dug their friends and families out of the rubble with their bare hands while sharing what little food and water they had.

Dany was criticized by some Canadian journalists for leaving Haiti after the earthquake. He should have stayed with his people, they said. And I have no doubt that if he were a doctor, he would have. But at that time, his role was to bear witness and he did it beautifully, going on the radio and television and writing his essays of fifteen hundred words or less to add one more voice to our chorus of bereavement and paralyzing loss, a loss that is echoed in his 2009 novel *L'Énigme du Retour* (The Enigma of Return).

Published in Paris and Canada a year before the earthquake, the novel follows a Haitian Canadian writer who returns to Haiti after the death of his father. *L'Énigme du Retour* was the first novel I read after the earthquake. I devoured it in a few hours. Unlike many of Dany's other books, it wasn't funny. I didn't laugh. I cried. The novel, it turns out, is a love poem, a love song to a Haiti that no longer exists, the Haiti of before the earthquake, which I am already starting to idealize, the Haiti where—even during its most difficult times—homes, churches, schools, bookstores, libraries, art galleries, museums, movie theaters, and government buildings were still standing.

"What is certain," writes the novelist narrator, "is that I wouldn't have written like this if I had stayed there / Maybe I would not have written at all / Living outside of our countries, do we write to console ourselves?"

Suddenly, this stunning chronicle of a homecoming to a very recent Haiti feels like a historical novel. Then it hits me. From now on, there will always be the Haiti of before the earthquake and the Haiti of after the earthquake. And after the earthquake, the way we read and the way we write, both inside and outside of Haiti, will never be the same.

Daring again to speak for the collective, I will venture to say that perhaps we will write with the same fervor and intensity (or even more) as before. Perhaps we will write with the same sense of fearlessness or hope. Perhaps we will continue to create as dangerously as possible, but our muse has been irreparably altered. Our people, both inside and outside of Haiti, have changed. In ways that I am not yet fully capable of describing, we artists too have changed.

Twenty-three days after the earthquake, my first trip to Haiti is brief, too brief. A friend finds a last-minute cancellation on a relief plane. Another agrees to help my husband look after our young girls in Miami.

I arrive in Port-au-Prince at an airport with cracked walls and broken windows. The fields around the runway are packed with American military helicopters and planes. Past a card table manned by three Haitian immigration officers, a group of young American soldiers idle, cradling what seem like machine guns. Through an arrangement between the Haitian and the U.S. governments, the American military, as leader in the relief effort, has taken over Toussaint L'Ouverture Airport.

Outside the airport, my friend Jhon Charles, a painter, and my husband's uncle, whom we call Tonton Jean, are waiting for me. A small man, Tonton Jean still cuts a striking figure with the dark motorcycle helmet he wears everywhere now to protect himself from falling debris. Jhon and Tonton Jean are standing behind a barricade near where the Americans have set up a Customs and Border Protection operation at the airport.

Whose borders are they protecting? I wonder. I soon get my answer. People with Haitian passports are not being allowed to enter the airport.

Maxo's oldest son, Nick, who now lives in Canada, is also in Haiti. He arrived a few days before I did to pay his respects and see what he could do for his brothers and sisters, who had been pulled, some of them wounded, from the rubble of the family house in Bel Air. When I arrive in Port-au-Prince, Nick is at the General Hospital with two of his siblings, getting them follow-up care.

One of the boys, thirteen-year-old Maxime, has already lost a toe to gangrene. Nick was told that his eight-year-old sister, Monica, might need to have her foot amputated, but the American doctors who are taking care of her in a tent clinic in the yard of Port-au-Prince's main hospital think they may be able to save her foot. This makes Monica luckier than a lot of other people I see hobbling on crutches all over Port-au Prince, their newly amputated limbs covered by shirt or blouse sleeves or pant legs carefully folded and pinned with large safety pins.

I am heading to the hospital to see Nick and the children when I get my first view of the areas surrounding my old neighborhood. Every other structure, it seems, is completely or partially destroyed. The school I attended as a girl is no more. The national cathedral, where my entire school was brought to attend mass every Friday, has collapsed. The house of the young teacher who tutored me when I fell behind in school has caved in, with most of her family members inside. The Lycée Petion, where generations of Haitian men had been educated, is gone. The Centre d'Art, which had nurtured thousands of Haitian artists, is barely standing. The Sainte-Trinité Church, where a group of famous Haitian artists had painted a stunning series of murals depicting the life of Christ, has crumbled, leaving only a section of a lacerated wall, where a wounded Christ seems to be ascending toward an open sky. Grand Rue, downtown Port-au-Prince's main thoroughfare, looks as though it had been bombed for several consecutive days. Standing in the middle of it reminds me of film I had seen of a destroyed Hiroshima. With its gorgeous white domes either tipped over or caved in, the national palace is the biggest symbol of the Haitian government's monumental loss of human and structural capital. Around the national palace has sprung up a massive tent city, filled with a patchwork of makeshift tents, actual tents, and semipermanent-looking corrugated tin structures, identical to those in dozens of other refugee camps all over the capital. The statues and monuments of the unknown maroon, a symbol of Haiti's freedom from slavery, of Toussaint L'Ouverture, Henri Christophe, Jean-Jacques Dessalines, and even a more recent massive globelike sculpture commissioned by President Jean-Bertrand Aristide to commemorate Haiti's bicentennial in 2004—these monuments and symbols around the national palace are still standing; however, their platforms now serve as perches from which people bathe and children play.

Outside the nursing and midwifery schools near the General Hospital are piles of human remains freshly pulled from the rubble. Dense rings of flies surround them. The remains are stuck together in two large balls. I wonder out loud whether all these nursing and midwifery students had been embracing one other when the ceiling collapsed on top of them, their arms and legs crisscrossed and intertwined. My friend Jhon Charles corrects me.

"These are all body parts," he says, "legs and arms that were pulled out the rubble and placed on the side of the road, where they dried further and melded together." Sticking to several of the flesh-depleted legs are pieces of yellowed cloth—skirts, I realize, which many of the women must have been wearing.

Across the street from the remains, people line up to watch. One woman pleads with the crowd to repent. "Call on Jesus! He is all we have left."

"We are nothing," another man says, while holding a rag up against his nose. "Look at this, we are nothing."

Jhon is a lively thirty-four-year-old who under normal circumstances has an easy laugh. He has been drawing and painting since he was a boy, using up leftover materials from his artist father. Later he attended Haiti's National School of the Arts, and he has been painting and teaching art in secondary schools since he graduated. Even though he is at the beginning of his career, he has already participated in group shows in Port-au-Prince, New York, Miami, and Caracas, Venezuela. Jhon grew up in Carrefour, where Tonton Jean also lives. The epicenter of the earthquake was near Carrefour. A week after the earthquake, my husband and I were still trying to locate Jhon and Tonton Jean. Their cell phones were not working and, besides, they were both very busy. Tonton Jean was pulling people out of the rubble and Jhon was teaching the traumatized children in the tent city near his house to draw.

In the tent clinic at the general hospital, I find Maxo's son Maxime, sleeping on a bench near where Maxime's sister Monica is attached to an antibiotic drip. All around Monica, wounded adults and children lie on their sides or backs on military cots. Most of the adults have vacant stares, while the children look around half curious, examining each new person who walks in. I try to imagine what it must have been like in this tent and others like it during those first days after the earthquake, when, Tonton Jean tells me, people were showing up at the little clinic across the street from his house in Carrefour, without noses and ears or arms and legs.

In the tent clinic I say hello to Monica. She looks up at me and blinks but otherwise does not react. Her eyes are dimmed and it appears that she may still be in shock. To watch your house and neighborhood, your city, crumble, then to watch your father die, and then nearly to die yourself, all before your tenth birthday, seems like an insurmountable obstacle for any child.

Even before this tragedy, Monica was a shy girl. When I saw her during my visits to Haiti, she would speak to me only when she was told what to say. The same was true when I spoke to her on the phone. Now in the tent clinic, I give her a kiss in the middle of her head, where her hair has been shaved in an uneven line to place a bandage where a piece of cement had split open her scalp.

Before I leave the tent hospital, the blonde young American doctor who is taking care of Monica gives her a yellow smiley-face sticker.

"She's my brave little soldier," the doctor says.

I thank her in English.

"You speak English very well," she says, before moving to the severely dehydrated baby in the next cot.

My next family stop is in Delmas, to see my Tante Zi. Though it had not collapsed, her house, perched on a hill above a busy street, is too cracked to be habitable, so she is staying in a large tent city in an open field nearby. We had talked often after the earthquake, and her biggest fear was of being caught out there in the rain. I had pleaded with her to go to La Plaine, where we had other family members, but she did not want to leave her damaged house, fearing that it might be vandalized or razed while she was gone.

When I reach Tante Zi's house, some of the family members from La Plaine, including NC, are there too. We are too afraid to go inside the house, so we all gather on the sidewalk out front, which is lined with tents and improvised showers. It astounds me how much more of Haitian life now takes place outside, the most intimate interactions casually unfolding before our eyes: a girl sitting between her boyfriend's legs on a car hood, a woman bathing her elderly mother with a bowl and a bucket. These are things we might have seen before, but now they are reproduced in some variation in front of dozens of shattered or nearly shattered houses on almost every street.

I hug NC and Tante Zi and six of my other cousins and four of their children. They tell me about the others. The cousin with the broken back may possibly be airlifted out of the country. The others from La Plaine were still sleeping outside their house but through a contact in Port-au-Prince they had gotten some water. Everyone had received the money the family had put together and wired them for food. Through all this, we hold and cradle one another, and while I hand them the tents and tarp they had requested, I start repeating something I hear Tonton Jean say each time he runs into a friend.

"I'm glad you're here. I'm glad *bagay la*—the thing—left you alive so I can see you."

Bagay la, this thing that different people are calling different things, this thing that at that moment has no official name. This thing that Tonton Jean calls Ti Roro, after a boy who used to bully him when he was young; that Jhon calls Ti Rasta for the same reason; that people on several radio program are calling Goudougoudou.

"I am glad Goudougoudou left you alive so I can see you," I say.

They laugh and their laughter fills me with more hope than the moment deserves. But this is really all I have come for. I have come to embrace them, the living, and I have come to honor the dead.

They show me their scrapes and bruises and I hug them some more, until my body aches. I take pictures for the rest of the family. I know everyone will be astounded by how well they look, how beautiful and well put together in their impeccable clothes. I love them so much. I am so proud of them.

Still, I ask myself how long they can live the way they are living, out in the open, waiting.

Two of them have tourist visas to Canada and the United States, but they stay because they cannot leave the others, who are mostly children. NC does not have a visa. She wants a student visa, to continue her accounting studies abroad. She hands me a manila envelope filled with documents, her birth certificate, her report cards, her school papers. She gives them to me for safekeeping, but also so I can see what I can do to get her out of the country.

NC, like many of my family members in Haiti, has always overestimated my ability to do things like this, to get people out of bad situations. I hope at that moment that she is right. I hope I can help. I have sometimes succeeded in helping, but mostly I have failed. Case in point: my elderly uncle died trying to enter the United States. I could not save him.

I sleep in Carrefour to be closer to the town of Léogâne, where a few of my maternal cousins still live. Something close to 90 percent of the structures in Léogâne were destroyed in the earthquake, including a small pharmacy run by a young couple I know, both of whom were killed when their building crumpled on top of them. While driving through Léogâne one morning, Jhon and I spot, past a cardboard sign with a plea for food in the entryway of a makeshift refugee camp, a large white tent with a striking image painted on it: a stunningly beautiful chocolate angel with her face turned up toward an indigo sky as she floats over a pile of muddied corpses.

Jhon leaps out of the car to have a better look.

Misty-eyed, he whispers, "Like Picasso and *Guernica* after the Spanish Civil War. We will have our Guernica."

"Or thousands of them," I concur.

Miraculously, my maternal grandmother's house, the house where I spent parts of my summer vacations as a girl, is still standing. It had been rebuilt some years back, cement blocks replacing the wooden walls and tin roof I knew and loved. The outer wall around the property has collapsed. As has the house that my cousin Eli and his wife had recently bought a few feet away.

Since the earthquake, they had already built a tiny two-room house with wooden walls and a tin roof and a narrow porch in the middle of an open field in an area named Cité Napoléon, after my mother's family. Eli's new house looks like my grandmother's old house, the one I'd loved.

Some time later, my last stop, before leaving Haiti, is at the compound in Bel Air where Maxo and his wife and children had been living. There is the church, my uncle's chef d'oeuvre, which had been built nearly forty years earlier at street level and had cement walls and a triangular metal roof. Underneath the church, in a kind of basement that was on the same level as another street, were the classrooms for a small school. Behind the church was the two-level apartment where Maxo and his family lived. Over the years, Maxo had added two more stories and a few small rental apartments to the complex. During the earthquake, all of that crumbled and, when he was running from the street where his car was parked to the apartment where his wife and children were found, fell on top of him and the others.

No one is sure where Maxo's son Nozial was, but it is believed that he had been playing where the rubble is most impenetrable, where all four stories piled up. Because Maxo was running when the building collapsed, he may have jumped or crawled into a place that made it easier to find his remains. The pile of rubble on top of the others made it impossible to extract theirs.

When I enter the church during my visit, I am amazed how little damage it appears to have sustained. Given that so many buildings around it had crumbled, its endurance seems part of some greater design, like the twenty-foot crucifix standing in the ruins of the collapsed Sacré-Cœur Church in the Turgeau neighborhood of Port-au-Prince.

The church is open and a group of men are huddled in the aisle in deep conversation when I walk in. One of them offers to show me Maxo's makeshift grave.

I descend a cracked cement staircase, seeing through the fallen basement walls the foundations of the two houses on either side of me. It occurs to me that I am in a cavernous hole around which the earthquake crumpled everything else. Through the gaps in the wall I can see parts of the bottom of the rubble.

The danger of my being there suddenly hits home. So quickly, more quickly than I would have liked, I kiss my hand and then bend down and touch the cemented mound where Maxo had been buried.

Esther, the maternal cousin who had overseen his burial, had carved in the cement his name, his date of birth, and the day that he died, the day that so many died.

"We buried him there and I marked it," she had told me on the phone, "so that whenever any of you come back from *lòt bò dlo*, you can see and touch his grave."

I reach down and touch the grave again. I feel that I should perhaps say more prayers, intone more words, but frankly I am afraid. A massive church is resting on a shattered foundation around me. Should there be another aftershock, I could be crushed.

"Good-bye, Maxo," I simply say. "Good-bye, Nozial."

Emerging from under the church and into the sunlight, I remember thinking, each time I saw someone rescued from the rubble on television, that it looked a lot like a vaginal birth, the rescue teams nudging, like midwives, a head, then a shoulder, then some arms, and then some legs, out of the expanded earth.

Maxo and Nozial, I thought, were never reborn.

At Toussaint L'Ouverture Airport, I must show my American passport to get inside to meet the plane for the return trip. The first U.S. Customs and Border Protection officer at the airport entrance asks me to take off my glasses as he looks at my picture on the passport. He holds the passport up to the sunlight for some time to verify that it is not fake. I am embarrassed and slightly humiliated, but these, I suppose, are lesser humiliations compared to what my loved ones and so many others are going through. The second and third Customs and Border Protection officers are Haitian Americans who speak to me in Creole. They wish me a good return trip "home."

On the plane, I listen quietly as the flight attendant thanks the doctors and nurses who are returning to the United States from stints as volunteers in Haiti.

"I bet you're looking forward to hot showers and warm beds and U.S. ice," she says.

The doctors and others clap and whistle in agreement.

"Well," she says, "I can offer you one of those things. The U.S. ice."

Wrapping up, she adds, "God bless America."

Feeling overly protective of an already battered Haiti, I hear myself cry out, "God bless Haiti, too," drawing a few stares from my fellow passengers.

The man in the seat behind me taps me on the shoulder and says, "Really. God bless both America and Haiti."

As we take off, I look down at the harbor, where a U.S military helicopter is flying between Toussaint L'Ouverture Airport and the USNS *Comfort* medical ship anchored just outside Port-au-Prince harbor. Further out to sea are U.S. Coast Guard ships, whose primary purpose is to make sure that Haitians are intercepted if they try to get on boats and head to the United States.

I have a copy of *Les Nègres* that I had meant to leave on Maxo's grave under the church, but in my haste and fear I had forgotten and brought it back with me.

I turn my eyes from the Coast Guard ships, and now on the plane I open the book and begin reading, turning immediately to the page that, soon after I'd learned of Maxo's death, had directly spoken to me: "Your song was very beautiful, and your sadness does me honor. I'm going to start life in a new world. If ever I return, I'll tell you what it's like there. Great black country, I bid thee farewell."

Great black country, I too bid thee farewell, I think.

At least for now.

A Year and a Day

In the Haitian Vodou tradition, it is believed by some that the souls of the newly dead slip into rivers and streams and remain there, under the water, for a year and a day. Then, lured by ritual prayer and song, the souls emerge from the water and the spirits are reborn. These reincarnated spirits go on to occupy trees, and, if you listen closely, you may hear their hushed whispers in the wind. The spirits can also hover over mountain ranges, or in grottoes, or caves, where familiar voices echo our own when we call out their names. The year-and-a-day commemoration is seen, in families that believe in it and practice it, as a tremendous obligation, an honorable duty, in part because it assures a transcendental continuity of the kind that has kept us Haitians, no matter where we live, linked to our ancestors for generations.

By this interpretation of death, one of many in Haiti, more than two hundred thousand souls went *anba dlo*—under the water—after the earthquake on January 12, 2010. Their bodies, however, were elsewhere. Many, like Maxo's son Nozial, were never recovered and removed from the rubble of their homes, schools, offices, churches, or beauty parlors. Many were picked up by earth movers on roadsides and dumped into mass graves. Many were burned, like kindling, in bonfires, for fear that they might infect the living.

"In Haiti, people never really die," my aunts and grandmothers said when I was a child, which seemed strange, because in Haiti people were always dying. They died in disasters both natural and man-made. They died from political violence. They died of infections that would have been easily treated elsewhere. They even died of chagrin, of broken hearts. But what I didn't fully understand was that in Haiti people's spirits never really die. This has been proved true in the stories I have seen and read since the earthquake, of boundless suffering endured with grace and dignity: mothers have spent nights standing knee-deep in mud, cradling their babies in their arms, while rain pounded the tarpaulin above their heads; amputees have learned to walk, and even dance, on their new prostheses within hours of getting them; rape victims have created organizations to protect other rape victims; people have tried, in any way they could, to reclaim a shadow of their past lives.

My aunts and grandmothers were also talking about souls, which never really die, even when the visual and verbal manifestations of their transition—the tombstones and mausoleums, the elaborate wakes and church services, the *desounen* prayers that encourage the body to surrender the spirit, the mourning rituals of all religions—become a luxury, like so much else in Haiti, like a home, like bread, like clean water.

In the year following the earthquake, Haiti lost some 5,000 people to cholera, an epidemic that is born out of water. This epidemic, which was introduced and spread throughout the country by insufficient sanitation conditions at the Mirebalais MINUSTAH camp—a facility used by several hundred Nepalese troops—could potentially take up to eight hundred thousand lives, quadrupling the estimated number of deaths during the earthquake. And with the contagion of cholera comes a stigma that follows one even in death. People cannot touch a loved one who has died of cholera. No ritual bath is possible, no last dressing of the body. There are only more mass graves.

In the emerging lore and reality of cholera, water, this fragile veil between life and death for so many Haitians, has become a feared poison. In Haiti's Artibonite Valley—the country's breadbasket—rice farmers refused to step into the bacteria-infected waters of their paddies, setting the stage for potential food shortages and more possible death ahead, this time from hunger. In the precarious dance for survival, in which we long to honor the dead while still harboring the fear of joining them, will our rivers and streams even be trusted to shelter and then return souls?

In the days following January 12, 2010, while watching the crumbled buildings and crushed bodies that were shown around the clock on American television, I thought that I was witnessing the darkest moment in Haiti's history. Then I heard one of the survivors say, either on radio or on television, that during the earthquake it was as if the earth had become liquid, like water. That's when I began to imagine them, all these thousands and thousands of souls, slipping into the country's rivers and streams, then waiting out their year and a day before reemerging and reclaiming their places among us. And, briefly, I was hopeful.

My hope came not only from the possibility of their and our communal rebirth but from the extra day that would follow the close of a most terrible year. That extra day guarantees nothing, except that it will lead us into the following year, and the one after that, and the one after that.

ACKNOWLEDGMENTS

I am extremely grateful to the magnificent Toni Morrison for her kindness in having me present the second annual Toni Morrison lecture (March 2008), which led to this book. Thanks also to Eddie Glaude, Joelle Loessy, Valerie Smith, Chang Rae Lee, and Fred Appel for their assistance. And to Cornel West, the standard bearer. At last I have an opportunity to thank Marcel Duret for his promotion of Haitian culture in Japan and the enjoyable and informative trips there. Thanks also to Patricia Benoit, Fedo Boyer, Jim Hanks, Nicole Aragi, Kathie Klarreich, Project MediShare, Kimberly Green, and the Green Family Foundation. My thanks also to Daniel Morel for his time and his work. My deepest gratitude to the John D. and Catherine T. MacArthur Foundation. Thanks lastly, to Pascale Monnin for the art used on the book cover.

Some of the chapters in this book appeared previously in the following publications:

Chapter 2 is taken partially from "A Taste of Coffee" in *Calabash* (May 2001). Other material is from an afterword to *Breath, Eyes, Memory*, by Edwidge Danticat (Random House Inc., 1999).

ACKNOWLEDGMENTS

Chapter 3 is taken partially from *The Butterfly's Way: Voices from the Haitian Dyaspora in the United States*, edited by Edwidge Danticat (Soho Press, 2003). Other material is from the article "Bonjour Jean" in *The Nation* (February 19, 2001).

Chapter 4 is taken partially from the foreword to *Memoir of an Amnesiac* by J. Jan Dominique (Caribbean Studies Press, 2008). Other material is from the introduction to *Love, Anger, Madness* by Marie Vieux-Chauvet (Random House, Inc., 2009).

Chapter 6 is taken partially from the essay "Out of the Shadows" in *The Progressive* (June 2006).

Chapter 7 is taken partially from in the article "Thomas Jefferson: The Private War: Ignoring the Revolution Next Door" in *Time* (July 05, 2004). Other material is from the introduction to *The Kingdom of This World*, by Alejo Carpentier (Farrar, Straus and Giroux, 2006).

Chapter 8 is taken partially from the essay "Another Country" in *The Progressive* (Fall 2005).

Chapter 9 is taken partially from the article "On Borrowed Wings" in *The Telegraph India* (October 2004).

Chapter 12 is taken partially from the article "A Little While" in the *New Yorker* (February 1, 2010). Other material is taken partially from the article "Aftershocks: Bloodied, shaken—and beloved" in the *Miami Herald* (January 17, 2010).

The Postscript is taken, in slightly different form, from the article "A Year and a Day" in *The New Yorker* (January 17, 2011).

NOTES

Chapter 1. Create Dangerously

Daniel Morel and Jane Regan of Wozo Productions provided the footage of Marcel Numa and Louis Drouin referred to in this chapter. Louis Drouin's final statement was published in Prosper Avril, *From Glory to Disgrace: The Haitian Army, 1804–1994* (Parkland, FL: Universal Publishers, 1999). "Create Dangerously," Albert Camus' lecture, which was delivered at the University of Uppsala in December 1957, as *L'Artiste et son temps*, is reprinted in *Resistance, Rebellion, and Death* (New York: Vintage International, 1995.) The *Le Matin* quotation is from Bernard Diederich and Al Burt, *Papa Doc: The Truth about Haiti Today* (New York: McGraw-Hill, 1969). All Ralph Waldo Emerson quotations are from *Ralph Waldo Emerson: Selected Essays, Lectures and Poems*, edited and with a foreword by Robert D. Richardson (New York: Bantam Classics, 1990). The Roland Barthes quotation "a text's unity lies not in its origin but in its destination" is from the essay "The Death of the Author" in Image-Music-Text (New York: Hill and Wang, 1978) Translations from Dany Laferrière's *Je suis un écrivain japonais* (Paris: Grasset, 2008) and from Jan J. Dominique's *Mémoire errante* (Montreal: Mémoire d'encrier, 2007) were done by me. The "We have still not had a death" quotation from Gabriel Garcia Márquez's *One Hundred Years of Solitude* is from the Perennial Classics edition (New York: Harper, 1998). The Toni Morrison quotation paraphrased in this chapter is "What it is to live at the edge of towns that cannot bear your company," from Toni Morrison's Nobel lecture in literature delivered in Sweden on December 7, 1993, and printed in *The Nobel Lecture in Literature, 1993* (New York: Knopf, 1994). The quotations from Albert Camus' *Caligula* are from the book *Caligula and Three Other Plays* by Albert Camus (New York: Alfred A. Knopf, 1966). The quotations from Alice Walker are from *In Search of Our Mothers' Gardens: Womanist Prose* (New York: Harcourt Brace & Company, 1983).

NOTES

Chapter 3. I Am Not a Journalist

The Michèle Montas quotation "I was no longer willing to go to another funeral" is from an interview with Bob Garfield for *On the Media*, a segment titled "Haiti's Media Crisis," March 14, 2003. For a better understanding of Jean Dominique and Michèle Montas, see the documentary *The Agronomist*, directed by Jonathan Demme. The quotations from *Mémoire errante* (Montreal: Mémoire d'encrier, 2007) in this chapter and the others were translated by me.

Chapter 4. Daughters of Memory

The quotations from Marie Vieux-Chauvet's *Love, Anger, Madness* are from the translation by Rose-Myriam Réjouis and Val Vinokur (New York: Modern Library, 2009). The quotation by Rose-Myriam Réjouis is also from that edition. Jan J. Dominique's comments regarding Jacques Roumain are taken from her essay "Roumain et la dévoreuse de mots: L'adolescente et les livres," published in *Mon Roumain à Moi* (Port-au-Prince: Presses Nationales d'Haiti, 2007). The quotation from the essay was translated by me. The W.E.B. Dubois quotation starting "The United States is at war with Haiti" can be found in *W.E.B. Dubois: A Reader*, edited by David Levering Lewis (New York: Henry Holt, 1995).

Chapter 5. I Speak Out

Except where indicated, the Alèrte Bélance quotations are from Beverly Bell, *Walking on Fire: Haitian Women's Stories of Survival and Resistance* (Ithaca, NY: Cornell University Press, 2001). The quotations from and references to Toni Morrison's *Beloved* are from the Vintage International edition (New York: Vintage, 1987).

Chapter 7. Bicentennial

The Thomas Jefferson quotations can be found at the Library of Congress's American Memory Archives: The Thomas Jefferson Papers 1606–1827 at http://memory.loc.gov/ammem/collections/jefferson_papers. I also use *Notes on the State of Virginia*, edited by William Peden (Chapel Hill: University of North Carolina Press, 1982). Toussaint L'Ouverture's speech that begins

"In overthrowing me . . . " is widely circulated and paraphrased. I am using the version that is in Ralph Korngold, *Citizen Toussaint* (Westport, CT: Greenwood Press, 1979). For a recent biography of Toussaint L'Ouverture, see Madison Smartt Bell, *Toussaint Louverture: A Biography* (New York: Pantheon Books, 2007). The edition of Alejo Carpentier's *Kingdom of This World* referenced and quoted here was published by Farrar, Straus and Giroux in 2006. Alejo Carpentier's comments about Haiti and magic realism were reprinted in Cristina Garcia, ed., *Cubanisimo: The Vintage Book of Contemporary Cuban Literature* (New York: Vintage, 2003)

Chapter 8. Another Country

The quotation from *Their Eyes Were Watching God* is from the Harper Collins Perennial edition (New York: Harper Collins, 1999.) The Masood Farivar quotation is from his essay "Man on the Path," in *110 Stories: New York Writes after September 11*, edited by Ulrich Baer (New York: New York University Press, 2002). The Isabel Allende quotation is from *My Invented Country: A Nostalgic Journey through Chile*, translated by Margaret Sayers Peden (New York: Harper Collins, 2003).

Chapter 9. Flying Home

The Wole Soyinka poem "New York, USA" is from *Mandela's Earth and Other Poems* (New York: Random House, 1988.) "i have not written one word / no poetry in the ashes south of canal street" is from the poem "first writing since" by Suheir Hammad published in *Trauma at Home: After 9/11*, edited by Judith Greenberg (Lincoln: University of Nebraska Press, 2003.) The Ralph Ellison short story "Flying Home" is found in the book *Flying Home*, edited by John F. Callahan (New York: Vintage International, 1996). The quotation "On Wednesday the 18th of February, 1931, I will take off from Mercy and fly away on my own wings. Please forgive me, I loved you all" is from Toni Morrison's *Song of Solomon* (New York: Vintage International, 1977.) The Ralph Waldo Emerson quotations here are from the essay "The Poet" in *Ralph Waldo Emerson: Selected Essays, Lectures and Poems*, edited and with a foreword by Robert D. Richardson (New York: Bantam Classics, 1990). The Adrian Dannat quotation concerning Michael Richards is from Michael Richards's obituary in the *Independent* on September 24, 2001. The

Moukhtar Kocache quotation is from C. Carr, "Lost Horizons: An Artist Dead, a Downtown Arts Organization in Ruins," *Village Voice*, September 18, 2001. The quote from Assotto Saint is from *Spells of a Voodoo Doll: The Poems, Fiction, Essays and Plays of Assotto Saint* (New York, Richard Kasak Books, 1996).

Chapter 10. Welcoming Ghosts

For much of Hector Hyppolite's life story, I am grateful to Selden Rodman's *The Miracle of Haitian Art* (Garden City, NY: Doubleday, 1974) as well as Selden Rodman's *Where Art Is Joy, Haitian Art: The First Forty Years* (New York: Ruggles de Latour, 1988). Basquiat's biography, particularly his "Papa, I will be very famous one day," is from Phoebe Hoban's *Basquiat: A Quick Killing in Art* (Harmondsworth, UK: Penguin, 1998). Demosthenes Davvetas's interview with Jean-Michel Basquiat was published in *New Art International*, no. 3 (October–November 1998), and was reprinted in the art catalog *Basquiat* (Milan: Edizioni Charta and Civico Museo Revoltella Trieste, 1999). The Miller/Basquiat interview (*Jean-Michel Basquiat: An Interview*, ART/new york, no. 30A, 1989) is from Inner Tube Video. The "Madison Avenue Primitive" reference is from Adam Gopnik, "Madison Avenue Primitive," *New Yorker*, November 9, 1992.

Chapter 11. Acheiropoietos

The poem "Tourist" by Felix Morisseau-Leroy was translated from Haitian Creole by Jack Hirschman and is published widely on the Internet as well as in *Haitiad and Oddities*, edited by Jeffrey Knapp (Austin: University of Texas, 1991). The Junot Díaz quotation is from his essay "Becoming a Writer," published in *O: The Oprah Magazine*, November 2009. Selden Rodman and Carole Cleaver tell a version of the story about Gran Brigit and the cemetery tree in their book *Spirits of the Night: The Vaudun Gods of Haiti* (Dallas: Spring Publications, 1992). The Susan Sontag quotations are from Susan Sontag, *On Photography* (New York: Farrar, Strauss, Giroux, 1973). The Roland Barthes quotations are from Roland Barthes, *Camera Lucida: Reflections on Photography*, translated by Richard Howard (New York: Farrar, Strauss, Giroux, 1973). Jane Regan and Daniel Morel's book on the Septentrional has not yet been published. The quotations are from a manuscript in progress. Albert Camus' short story "The Artist at Work" (originally "Jonas ou l'artiste au travail") is reprinted in Albert Camus, *The Plague, The Fall, Exile and the Kingdom, and Selected Essays* (New York: Everyman's Library, 2004).

Chapter 12. Our Guernica

The Jean Genet quotation, "Your song was very beautiful," is from the English edition of Jean Genet's *Les Nègres—The Blacks* (New York: Grove Press, 1960). The Dolores Dominique Neptune quotations are from an e-mail message dated January 30, 2010, sent by Claudine Michel, Professor, Department of Black Studies, University of California, Santa Barbara. The Evelyne Trouillot quotation is from Evelyne Trouillot, "Aftershocks," Op-ed, *New York Times*, January 20, 2010. The Lyonel Trouillot quotation is from Lyonel Trouillot, "Carnet de Bord à Haiti: Fais divers de nos mauvais jours, 5/9," published on January 24, 2010, at www.lepoint.fr; the translation is mine.

INDEX